SEEING THROUGH THE SYSTEM

SEEING THROUGH THE SYSTEM:
The Invisible Class Struggle in America

GUS J. BAGAKIS
with a preface by Douglas Dowd

iUniverse, Inc.
Bloomington

SEEING THROUGH THE SYSTEM
THE INVISIBLE CLASS STRUGGLE IN AMERICA

Copyright © 2013 Gus Bagakis.

All rights reserved. No part of this book may be used or reproduced by any means, graphic, electronic, or mechanical, including photocopying, recording, taping or by any information storage retrieval system without the written permission of the publisher except in the case of brief quotations embodied in critical articles and reviews.

iUniverse books may be ordered through booksellers or by contacting:

iUniverse
1663 Liberty Drive
Bloomington, IN 47403
www.iuniverse.com
1-800-Authors (1-800-288-4677)

Because of the dynamic nature of the Internet, any web addresses or links contained in this book may have changed since publication and may no longer be valid. The views expressed in this work are solely those of the author and do not necessarily reflect the views of the publisher, and the publisher hereby disclaims any responsibility for them.

Any people depicted in stock imagery provided by Thinkstock are models, and such images are being used for illustrative purposes only.

Certain stock imagery © Thinkstock.

ISBN: 978-1-4759-9135-2 (sc)
ISBN: 978-1-4759-9134-5 (hc)
ISBN: 978-1-4759-9133-8 (e)

Library of Congress Control Number: 2013908750

Printed in the United States of America.

iUniverse rev. date: 6/20/2013

Dedicated to the memories of

Judith Ann Bagakis
Ricky Sherover-Marcuse
Sabi Guerra
Sid Efross
Bob Wendlinger
Gerti

Differences in class, in social and economic power, in educational opportunity and achievement, in health and physical well being, are the expression and result of institutionalized inequalities in opportunity. Such differences perpetuate and increase the social imbalances in power and thereby serve to maintain all forms of oppression.
—Erica Sherover-Marcuse

The system is not simply an external set of relations between people and things. It infects subjectivity. It manufactures consent, through force and fear, but largely through the representations with which it infects the mind. It must at all costs conceal the truth that a better world is possible. It is, by its very nature, a living lie. The untruth of daily life is so pervasive it easily escapes notice. In order for the truth to emerge, the false representations must be destroyed. The world must be shaken and shocked into revelation.
—Osha Neumann

The corporate core of the American economy will not tolerate any basic shift away from the growth-gripped, energy-guzzling, consumption-crazed system that has made it so wealthy and powerful. Significant reforms will be made only when corporate power is confronted with substantial public resistance, and radical new alternatives will not gain popular support until a critical mass of Americans considers the established order so bankrupt and broken they are willing to rise up and replace it.
—Craig Collins

The truly central and demanding question is obviously this: If most of what we have today is attributable to knowledge advances that we all inherit in common, why, specifically, should this gift of our collective history not more generously benefit all members of society? The top 1 percent of US households now receives far more income than the bottom 150 million Americans combined. The richest 1 percent of households owns nearly half of all investment assets (stocks and mutual funds, financial securities, business equity, trusts, nonhome real estate). A mere 400 individuals at the top have a combined net worth greater than the bottom 60 percent of the nation taken together. If America's vast wealth is mainly a gift of our common past, how, specifically, can such disparities be justified?

—Gar Alperovitz

TABLE OF CONTENTS

Preface xi
Acknowledgments xiii
Introduction xv
    A Personal Statement xv
    Social Class Questionnaire (excerpt) xix
    What Happened to Class? xx
    The Plan of This Book xxv

Chapter 1 The System: Capitalism 1
    The Mainstream Perspectie 3
    The Class Analysis Perspective 4
    Why Is Capitalism Not Understood or Paid Attention To? 6
    Capitalism from the Working-Class Perspective: A Summary 9

Chapter 2 A Working Definition of Class 10
    The Mainstream Definition of Class 11
    The Working-Class Definition of Class 12
    How Did Capitalism Arise? 16
    Summary 24
    Definitions Have Consequences 25

Chapter 3 What Is Class Analysis? 29
    Why Class Analysis Is Important 31
    Studying Class: Groups, Not Individuals 33
    Production: The Heart of Class Analysis 34

Chapter 4 The Question about the Middle Class 38
    Why Is It Hard to Drop the Concept "Middle Class"? 41
    How Do "Coordinators" Differ from the Working Class? 45

Chapter 5 The Ruling Class 50
   What about Small Business? 60

Chapter 6 The Excluded and Abused Workers 63
   What Is the Underclass? 65
   What about Gender and Race? 67
   Some Historical Examples 69
   What about the Disrespect of Common People? 71

Chapter 7 Unions 80

Chapter 8 The International Class Struggle and Globalization 91

Chapter 9 Class Analysis in the Coming Age of Energy Decline 99
   Capitalism with an Energy Focus 102
   A Short History: From Production to Catabolic Capitalism 104
   The Energy Problems for the Working Class: Addiction and Finitude ... 106
   The Danger of Denial: Complexity and EROEI (Energy Returned on Energy Invested) 109
   What Is the Working Class to Do? 112

Appendix 1 Social Class Questionnaire (complete) 119

Appendix 2 The Working Class and the Current Crisis of Capitalism 123
   The System—Capitalism (The Secondary Economy) 126
   How This Crisis Happened 130
   Tertiary Economy 132
   Primary Economy 135

Glossary 139

Bibliography 155

Index 173

Endnotes 177

PREFACE

Soon after Gus Bagakis finished the manuscript for this book, he sent me a copy, asking for my comments. We had known each other years before, when he was a student in one of my classes and since then had become a teacher himself. His students are very fortunate.

I have been teaching, reading, and writing economics and economic history now for sixty years; I can say without hesitation that *Seeing through the System* not only does what its title proposes but does so more clearly, interestingly, and substantially than any of the hundreds of books of socioeconomic analysis I have read in that long experience.

Put differently, I say without hesitation that what he has done is a masterpiece of teaching in the work's structure, content, and style. First, structure: it is unique in its way of proceeding within and between chapters—systematic assertions and explanations followed by equally systematic questions, answers, references, and abundant quotations. Next, content: the book's subtitle—*The Invisible Class Struggle in America*—is not only unique in itself but considerably more so in its substance, clarity, and strength. Style? Bagakis is an excellent writer in his clarity, content, and strength.

Taken together, the foregoing qualities provide a work that is not only powerful in its quality but also—rare in a textbook—gripping. Put differently, teachers who have the spirit and courage to provide their students with a work this probing and understanding of the status quo would soon find that their classrooms have become uniquely lively for all concerned.

I add this. We are living in a turbulent and fearful era, which reminds me of the 1930s (when I was in my teens). This work makes it possible for classes not only to become more interesting and lively but also assists young people to work for a safer, more sane, and more productive life.

—Douglas Dowd, visiting professor, University of Modena, Italy

ACKNOWLEDGMENTS

Thanks to the community who helped me write this book, especially to my students at San Francisco State University; my writing teachers Monza Naff and Andy Couturier; my friends and editors Bob Wendlinger and Russel Kilday-Hicks; my writing class; Sharon Ellison and Vicki Della Joio, my friends; Jerry Atkin, Terry Day, Craig Collins, Dick Adami, Sid Efross, John Chung, Robin Chang, Liz Raymer, Osha Neumann, Alex Pappas, and Yeshi Sherover-Neumann. Of course, I am responsible for any mistakes.

A special thanks to Dr. Craig Collins, who introduced me to the importance of fossil fuels and their relation to capitalism, class, climate change, and the earth's ecology.

INTRODUCTION

Unless one has placed oneself on the side of the oppressed, to feel with them, one cannot understand.
—Simone Weil

Years ago I recognized my kinship with all living things, and I made up my mind that I was not one bit better than the meanest on the earth. I said then and I say now, that while there is a lower class, I am in it; while there is a criminal element, I am of it; while there is a soul in prison, I am not free.
—Eugene V. Debs

A Personal Statement

In ancient Athens, Socrates said that the unexamined life is not worth living. I agree. We can examine our lives in numerous ways, but no examination would be complete today without including a class analysis. Class analysis is a powerful method that will give us insights into the nature of our personal and interpersonal experiences through an investigation into the structure of our society.

For most of my life, I knew something was wrong with the world around me. I saw too many instances in our rich country of people who were poor. My family, schools, churches, and other social institutions recited a multitude of justifications to explain that inequality.

- "Some people are simply lazy."
- "The way we are is God's plan; just accept it!"
- "Some people are luckier than others."
- "It's in the nature of some people to live like they do."
- "The poor have always been among us."
- "Some people are just smarter."
- "This is the way things are; it's the order of nature."

These justifications were not good enough for me. I met too many decent, smart, and hardworking poor people who deserved a better life. Eventually, I learned that, through class analysis, I could see that—for the most part—it was not a person's competence or incompetence or ambition or intelligence or luck that explained his or her fate but the way our society was organized and that poverty or wealth was an outcome of class difference, which was based on power.

After many years of working at all sorts of jobs—janitor, auto assembly-line worker, USAF ground radio repairman, aircraft mechanic, radio announcer, social worker, public school teacher, electronics repairman, and college lecturer—I came to believe that we need to create a society that supports the dignity and capacities of all people instead of beating them down and using them up. I also think that we cannot create a better society until we better understand this one, and class analysis will help bring us to that deeper understanding.

Understanding class analysis will not be easy. Individuals who bring up class differences have often been attacked for being radicals or rebels who are trying to stir up a class war in America (as if it didn't already exit). Because of its danger to the status quo, class analysis has been systematically ignored, distorted, or attacked by our media, government, business, and educational institutions. Another difficulty in promoting class analysis is responding to the resistance of those who have been raised and trained to believe there are no classes or that they and almost everyone else is a member of the middle class—another way of saying there are no classes. The final, most frustrating difficulty in promoting a class analysis was summarized by Upton Sinclair when he stated, "It is difficult to get a man to understand something when his salary depends on his not understanding it." But as critical thinkers, we need to persist and find out why class has been attacked or ignored and whose interests that serves.

As you begin this journey toward understanding class analysis, you may wonder if I, the author, am biased. I try to tell the truth based on facts that I present, but I recognize that a fact is an observation in terms of a perspective. My perspective is of the working class. That means I try to understand the world through the experiences of the working class. The glossary in this book defines some terms differently, based on the perspective of the class defining the term—working class or capitalist class (yes, reader, there is a capitalist class that owns most everything, unlike the working class that owns only their power to labor). Using a working-class perspective can be an odd experience, since most social research or history is not presented from the perspective of the working class. As Howard Zinn notes,

> ...the Preamble to the United States Constitution, which declares that "We the people" wrote this document, is a great deception. The Constitution was written in 1787 by fifty-five rich white men—slave owners, bondholders, merchants—who established a strong central government that would serve their class interests. That use of government for class purposes, to serve the needs of the wealthy and powerful, has continued throughout American history, down to the present day. It is disguised by language that suggests all of us, rich and poor and middle class have a common interest ... Class

interest has always been obscured behind an all-encompassing veil called "the national interest."[1]

In this book, I will be concerned with the things that were distorted or omitted with reference to our lives, the lives of working people. The information presented here is from the perspective of my education, my work history, my immigrant experience (my father emigrated from Crete in 1914), and the fact that everyone in my extended family labored at working-class jobs: as miners, manual laborers, in construction, as truck drivers, fruit pickers, in canneries, or industry. That history has put me in a position to be sensitive to the inequality and unfairness of wage labor. Although I am currently considered "middle class" given that I have been working as an adjunct college instructor for the past twenty years, I'm writing from the perspective of a Greek American working-class man educated in the American public schools—a structure designed to train the future workforce for our economy—who has experienced the anguish of the working class, that of being judged stupid and irrelevant and being made, for the most part, invisible in our society.

As I grew older, thanks to my work experience, some books, study groups, and a few friends and teachers, the class structure of our society became increasingly understandable to me. I was able to develop arguments and evidence that explained the world more clearly than the justifications given in my youth.

I believe that if you provisionally adopt a class analysis, as presented in this book, you will gain new, exciting insights about your position in society. Let's see if I'm right. First, I will begin by asking you to answer some questions about the meaning of class in your life. Later we will discuss the absence of class in the public realm and the definitions of class and class analysis.

Social Class Questionnaire (excerpt)[2]

Please respond to the following questions about social class. Before answering, talk to colleagues, friends, and family about your responses. Some who answered felt sad, because they uncovered painful family secrets; some said they saw the world and their relationships with friends and family differently. Some even said that these questions brought up issues that forced them to reframe their lives. In any event, by focusing on answers to these questions, you will probably trigger[3] memories of events in your life that you've forgotten about that can make a difference in the way you look at your world today. You may also find that the following questions are excellent dialogue starters for family gatherings, card nights, or any social functions.

a. How would you characterize your family's socioeconomic background (for example: poor, working class, lower middle class, middle class, upper middle class, ruling class)? What tells you this?

b. Pick five values/expectations/orientations that seem to be most valued in your family. Then pick five that seem to be least valued or important.

Getting by; making a moderate living; making a very good living; gaining social status or prominence; open communication among family members; going to a place of worship; keeping up with the neighbors; being physically fit or athletic; working out psychological issues through therapy; helping others; getting married and having children; respecting law and order; defending one's country; staying out of trouble with the law; being politically or socially aware; recognition; community service; saving money; making your money work for you; enjoying your money; getting a high school diploma; getting a college degree; getting an advanced or professional degree; learning a trade; helping to advance the cause of one's racial, religious, or cultural group; physical appearance; being a professional; being an entrepreneur; owning a home; being patriotic; going to private school; not being wasteful; having good etiquette.

c. Who does most of the work to keep your family functional? I'm not only referring to wage work but also the work of cleaning the house, washing clothes, shopping for food, cooking dinners, and caring for the children.

d. If money were not an issue, what work would you most want to do? Why? (The purpose of this question is to query whether most of us are spending our work time doing what we really want to do.)

I hope you can see by your answers to the above questions that class, although rarely discussed in our media, is of intense interest and importance. So why is it invisible?

What Happened to Class?

> *Most Americans have never seen the ignorance, degradation, hunger, sickness, and futility in which many other Americans live ... They won't become involved in economic or political change until something brings the seriousness of the situation home to them.*
> —Shirley Chisholm, six-term congresswoman, 1972 presidential candidate

In the 1930s, "class" was a common term. The country was in a depression. The class struggle between the working class and the capitalist class (the owners of industry) was a familiar theme. I remember growing up seeing newspaper and newsreel images of the Depression, with lines of gloomy workingmen in gray overcoats and gray hats lining up for food or applying for jobs. I remember seeing images of soot-smudged industrial plants with belching smokestacks, day after day swallowing up and spitting out exhausted workers dressed in striped, grimy overalls and carrying black lunch boxes. I remember the pictures of worn-out coal miners (my father was one of them) trudging out of the mines, covered with coal dust, with bright white eyes blankly staring out beneath their mining hats. I remember images of the parties of the rich with their jewels, flowing gowns, and black-and-white tuxedos standing before their mansions and expensive cars or the country clubs filled with frolicking "beautiful people" smiling and holding champagne glasses, posing for the newspapers.[4]

In contrast to that era, at the turn of the twenty-first century, class, which focused on the production process (factories), has been replaced in the public eye by a focus on consumption (shopping malls) and the era of advertising and status. Today, the clothing designating class is almost gone. For the most part, you can't see what class people belong to. Everyone looks the same. We almost all look "middle class"—bosses, mail clerks, secretaries, and account executives. The janitors, garbage men, maids, waitresses, and industrial employees have slipped into the background, ignored by the media, except when seen on the front pages of the corporate-controlled press as a menace to society during clashes around strikes.

The division between the workers and owners still exists, but it cannot be identified as in the stark contrasts of the past. The industrial plants have given way to glass skyscrapers, campuses, and pleasant business parks with lawns and flowers. We now mostly think of ourselves as being middle class, living in a global, corporate-dominated, postindustrial, and service or information society. The old industrial society has almost disappeared or has been exported to other countries.

Even though there are more people working today than during the 1930s, why does our society ignore class? Some proposed answers are the following:

1. Individuals' lives are no longer shaped by their work but by their lifestyles.
2. The United States at the end of World War II became an "affluent society," obscuring the sharp contrast between employees and owners.
3. The economy changed from industrial capitalism to finance capitalism, from the focus on profits through commodities to abstract financial transactions that create or destroy value.
4. Unions have been weakened and suffered catastrophic defeats.
5. Major industrial centers deindustrialized: Detroit, Chicago, Pittsburgh, Philadelphia, Baltimore, Trenton, Boston, and Saint Louis all lost hundreds of thousands of manufacturing jobs, beginning in the 1950s.
6. The working class disappeared partly due to the systematic antilabor bias of the media,[5] as well as its focus on other areas of life: business, celebrities, consumption, sports, politics, wars, technology, racism, and gender equality.
7. We have moved from the Industrial Revolution to the information revolution.
8. The workplace became automated and more skilled, well-educated technicians replaced the greasy blue-collar labor force.
9. Between the 1960s and 1990s, other social movements that seemed more relevant to the lives of the populace replaced class: civil rights, feminism, multiculturalism, ecology, gender equity, disability rights, AIDS, and immigrants' rights.
10. Blue-collar workers are portrayed as stereotypes like Ralph Kramden, Archie Bunker, and Homer Simpson. Who wants to identify with these buffoons?
11. Our culture's focus on individualism (the unconnected self) overlooks the power of the group (class).

12. Because of the focus on status, "working class" has become an offensive term today.

It seems that class vanished since it disappeared from the public's attention or was replaced by other areas of public concern. In this book, you will find that class did not disappear, but as Howard Zinn said, we have been trained to believe that "we mustn't talk of class division in this country ... We must believe we are one family—me and Exxon, you and Microsoft, the children of the CEOs and the children of the janitors. We must believe our interests are the same."[6]

A perspective that ignores class makes it difficult to define class. How do you define something that is not recognized? If you look at the *Statistical Abstract of the United States*, the yearly compilation of the official categories of information, you will find loads of interesting statistics but no figures that focus on class as defined here. The social sciences do not devote much effort in defining and studying something that is not officially sanctioned by grants and awards. But the awareness of class divisions is a reality for vast numbers of workers as well as the upper elites (although they don't discuss it in public). Still, class and class analysis are mysteries to many people in all sectors of our society. Let us see if we can help solve the mystery.

We also have an incorrect understanding of the meaning of class. Instead of defining class through vague determinations reflecting our narrow economic status—like income, how individuals dress, what they own, or how they are trained, educated, or cultured—we need to define class in a more precise way. This is accomplished when we see class as the relationship of one portion of the population to another in terms of their connection to the means of production (the land, forests, waters, mineral resources, raw materials, factories, corporations, means of transportation, and communication). The capitalist class owns the means of production, and the working class works with the means of production but does not own them. (This distinction will be expanded below.)

Today, although we cannot easily see them, the effects of class division still exist in the experiences of workers who complain about discrimination, boredom, the stupidity and insensitivity of the bosses, the purposelessness of their lives, the lack of decent public support structures for their families, and their constant struggle for money and security. It still exists where ordinary working people in factories, mines, fields, and offices are rebelling every day, trying to regain control over their lives while under the threat of being fired. It still exists because of the way factories or corporations are organized to create a perpetual conflict between employees and management over how production is carried out. It still exists, seeing that people are in fear of being fired. Management is always finding new ways of controlling and directing the workers, while workers are inventing new ways of defending themselves. This process of contention between the classes is called class struggle.

Today, the class struggle can be seen in the growing anger of the poor being left behind with little hope. This is due to the increasing division between the rich and the poor—the rich drive their BMWs and Mercedes-Benzes while the poor wait for buses.[7] Added to this is the recognition of the inability of our politicians to make things better.[8] People are starting to ask questions: Why am I poor even though I work hard? Why do some have extra money that they do not need? Why don't I have health care for my family? Why are people living in the streets? Why is there pollution in my neighborhood? Why don't I get what I need while my representatives in government are doing well themselves? Why are my children fighting and dying in foreign lands? Why is my neighborhood school failing? Why are so many black men in our prisons? Why are women not paid the same as men for doing the same work? Why are so few citizens voting or taking part in our civic life? Why is my community ignored? So many questions!

The Plan of This Book

In this book, you will be introduced to the tools you need to help you answer the above questions. Class never disappeared. We just lost track of it as society changed. Now, with the crises our nation is confronting, we are challenged to bring class back into public dialogue. We begin with a discussion of the system (capitalism) that pits one class against another. Chapter 2 will give a clear definition of class by contrasting it to the mainstream definition. Then we will move to a discussion of what a class analysis is in chapter 3. This shift will force us to explain, in chapter 4, what the middle class is and why—for the purposes of understanding the system—it is not a useful concept. In chapter 5, we turn to the ruling class, the historic enemy of the working class. Here you will get an overview and description of the power that the ruling capitalist class holds. Following this overview in chapter 6, we will move to the victims of that power: the excluded and abused workers, people of color, women, and the common people. Then, in chapter 7, we will turn to the union movement, the reaction to ruling class oppression. Chapter 8 will focus on the international scene and look at globalization and class. Chapter 9 will look to the near future and examine class analysis in the age of energy decline. Appendix 1 contains the full copy of the questionnaire about class. Appendix 2 concludes with a view of the current crisis of capitalism from the worker's perspective.

CHAPTER 1

The System: Capitalism

History suggests that capitalism is a necessary condition for political freedom.
—Milton Friedman

There must be something rotten in the very core of a social system which increases its wealth without diminishing its misery.
—Karl Marx, *New York Daily Tribune*, 1859

There are forty million poor people here, and one day we must ask the question, "Why are there forty million poor people in America?" And when you begin to ask that question, you are raising a question about the economic system, about a broader distribution of wealth. When you ask that question, you begin to question the capitalistic economy. And I'm simply saying that more and more, we've got to begin to ask questions about the whole society ... And you see, my friends, when you deal with this you begin to ask the question, "Who owns the oil?" You begin to ask the question, "Who owns the iron ore?" You begin to ask the question, "Why is it that people have to pay water

bills in a world that's two-thirds water?" These are words that must be said.
—Martin Luther King Jr.

In 1948, when I was ten years old, exploring the streets of downtown Oakland, California, I was shocked to see a man sprawled out facedown on the sidewalk. The populace passed by him, not paying any attention. Now, many years later, the homeless are common in the streets of Oakland as well as most of our major cities, and in the Oakland hills, where the rich live, the new houses are getting bigger. We have more homeless and bigger houses, and our prisons are overflowing. What happened? I believe the answer to these questions and others that involve inequality can be found through an understanding (that I call a class analysis) of our economic/social system—capitalism.

Capitalism is the dominant economy in our world. It began to develop in Europe in the late Middle Ages within the previous mode of production, feudalism[1]: an agricultural structure where serfs provided labor and military service to a lord in return for the use of his land. In the late Middle Ages, capitalism established a market[2] through the use of the very few workers who were not tied to the land as the serfs but who became tied through the wage system to the growing class of owners, called capitalists, who owned the factories, workplaces, and raw materials.

For the purpose of this book, I will reduce the numerous interpretations of capitalism to two: the mainstream and the class analysis. Although both perspectives describe the same system, they focus on different aspects of it, as you will see in the slight variations of the following definitions. The mainstream approach looks at capitalism from the top down, from the perspective of the winners: the owners, the bosses, and the heads of corporations who control the majority of wealth and power. This is the view that you are probably familiar with since most of the institutions in our society—the media, education, government, and business—promote it.

Class analysis looks at the capitalist system from the bottom up, from the perspective of the grass roots: of those who do the work, who are the poorest, and, at the same time, who are made invisible by the capitalist-controlled institutions of society (the newspapers, media, corporations, and educational systems).

For example: The mainstream perspective doesn't look upon class as a key feature of the capitalist system (other than including workers' wages in the costs of production). Look in any newspaper and check out the business section. Then look at the labor section. Oops, there is none![3] In contrast to the mainstream perspective, class analysis sees class as fundamental, as the motor of capitalism, but this perspective is only found in some alternative media.[4]

The Mainstream Perspectie

> *Capitalism is an economic system characterized by private or corporate ownership of capital goods, by investments that are determined by private decision, and by prices, production, and the distribution of goods that are determined mainly by competition in a free market.*
> —Merriam-Webster

The mainstream definition concentrates on the following: (1) private ownership and private decisions, (2) the competitive free markets, and (3) economics in the narrow sense—linking people with things (the focus is on products, profit, and growth). It is based on the assumptions that we are naturally competitive, greedy, and isolated. Most people who don't concern themselves with the way capitalism works or who see the capitalist system as natural, implicitly agree with this view of human nature. Do you? (Lots of people disagree with this view of human nature, but they are forced to act daily as isolated, competitive, greedy individuals in order to survive capitalism.)

In their praise of capitalism, mainstream advocates argue that it is the greatest arrangement for producing wealth. It has lifted millions from the hopeless lives of peasants into the modern office buildings and apartments of industrialized nations.

Mainstream advocates also argue that capitalism is based on the protection of the individual's right to life, liberty, and the pursuit of happiness. Free markets are founded on the individual's right to pursue a career, trade the products of his or her effort, and enjoy the wealth he or she has earned, without having to seek permission from others. Capitalism doesn't just make people wealthy; it affirms the freedom of the individual.

The top-down view misses the experience of those on the bottom. While this view sings the praises of the freedom of the individual, it ignores the fact that a small minority (capitalists) benefits while the rest of humanity suffers from war, racism, sexism, starvation, poverty, ill health, pollution, ecological catastrophe, and so on.[5]

The Class Analysis Perspective[6]

> Capitalism is a "socio-economic system where social relations [human relations] are based on commodities for exchange, in particular private ownership of production, and on the exploitation of wage labor."

The class analysis definition concentrates on the following: (1) workers as a group, (2) the fact that workers are exploited (exploitation occurs when one section of the population—the workers—produces a surplus that is controlled by the capitalists), and (3) economics in the larger sense—where the economy is viewed as part of a socioeconomic system that includes all aspects of human life, not just economic relationships. It is based on a different assumption about human nature: that we are interconnected social beings rather than isolated individuals in competition with one another.

An important distinction between the mainstream and the working-class perspective is seen in their understanding of the word "economics." Where the mainstream approach assumes economics is concerned with things, the working-class approach sees economics as concerned with relations that appear as things.[7] Michael Merrill, an American historian, addresses this distinction when he states that most historians mistakenly see capitalism as "just an economic system based on market exchange, private property, wage labor, and sophisticated financial instruments. A better approach would view capitalism as an arrangement of power relations that diverted the fruits of economic development into the hands of a small segment of society."[8]

Another way of saying this for the working class is that by selling our labor power to an employer, we turn ourselves into commodities. We throw away our humanity and become things, since—under capitalism—all transactions are carried on through the exchange of commodities. So under the mainstream perspective people are defined as being commodities, while under the working-class approach, we see that beneath commodities are social relations, human relations.

Class analysis recognizes that capitalism is a great advance over feudalism in that it is the first economic system that has created enough material wealth to potentially feed and clothe everyone. But the struggle between the very few capitalists and the mass of employees ends up with enormous inequalities: superrich capitalists and poor workers. This is because the capitalists own almost everything,[9] while the working class only owns its power to labor. Thus, the working class must work under capitalist-controlled conditions. If you own nearly everything and need employees to work for you, you have a great advantage over them (especially if you make it difficult for them to organize and struggle against your power by pitting subgroups of workers against one another through the use of racism, sexism, and ethnic strife).

This unequal relationship between capitalists and workers

can only be corrected when there are no classes and when workers democratically control their own production and produce goods based on need and not for profit.[10]

Class analysis is not only arguing for material fairness but also for employees to be treated like human beings, a demand that capitalism is incapable of meeting, because in creating wealth, the capitalist class must focus on profit, not use—on what makes the most money, not necessarily on what is most useful for the community. And workers are thrown into that process. They turn themselves into robots or zombies for capitalism by selling their labor power to the capitalists, thus losing control of their bodies. Worker-robots also don't see their work as part of their creative contribution to their community.

Under the mainstream perspective, employees have no say over their work and no control over their lives. The class analysis perspective argues that it is through labor, through our cooperative transformation of nature for our needs, that we become human beings.[11] This is why class analysis is in favor of overturning capitalism's class divisions and replacing them with a classless society that could lead to the creation of a social order where humans would become free to democratically control themselves in all areas of their lives. This is a truly revolutionary goal, for never before in human history have humans created a society in which all are free to fully develop themselves.

Why Is Capitalism Not Understood or Paid Attention To?

Most people do not understand capitalism as the arrangement that underlies and influences our daily lives. Both Frances Fitzgerald and James Loewen, in their studies of textbooks, found out that our educational system ignores class and the economy.[12] In addition, Michael Zweig, an economist and author,[13] being interviewed on the program *Class Dismissed*,[14] pointed out that PBS would not broadcast labor-funded films, because they considered them to be propaganda, but they would put on *Wall Street in Review*, funded by Merrill Lynch, since that show was judged as news. Zweig stated that the corporate funders behind PBS would not allow the terms "capitalism" or "capitalist class" on their broadcasts, although they would allow talk about the corporate elite or the "free" market. And if by some chance capitalism were talked about in the mass media, it would be presented from the mainstream perspective as a structure that ignores or minimizes the struggles of the workforce and maximizes the joy of consumerism and the values of individualism (I can "make it" by pulling myself up by my bootstraps).

Because of the public reaction to the 2008 crisis, the term "capitalism" has begun to enter the public conversation, especially among the traditionally critical alternative organizations. Generally, the mainstream discussions ignored the term. Frank Luntz, one of the Republican Party's chief messaging strategists, advocated at a Republican governor's association not to say "capitalism," because the American public thinks of it as an immoral arrangement. He proposed it be replaced by terms like "free market" or "economic freedom."[15] Still, as our economic crisis lengthens and deepens more people are looking up capitalism and socialism in the dictionary.[16]

What is it about the term "capitalism" that those in power are keeping from us? The best way for the capitalists to hide all of these facts is to hide the first one—that we live in a capitalist society,[17] which implies the following:

1. Capitalism (as defined by class analysis) reveals how our society works and who benefits and who suffers.
2. The rulers of our society own the means of production, distribution, and exchange, and they get the majority of the surplus created by the working class.
3. The government usually serves the capitalists' interests, due to the enormous lobbying and financial contributions that buy politicians.
4. The purpose of capitalism is to make profits. In doing this,

capitalists must give up as little of the surplus to the working class that actually generated it as possible. They do this by creating ways to replace workers with machines, technology, robots, and cheaper labor from other countries.
5. The conditions of life for the workforce are bad and getting worse. The rich are getting richer, and the poor are getting poorer.
6. Those who benefit from the present order of society have used their power and influence to cover up the above points.

The importance of capitalism dates from mercantilism and the era of European colonialism to the Industrial Revolution that began in the eighteenth century, when bankers, merchants, and industrialists began to displace landowners in political, economic, and social importance. Since those days, capitalism has taken numerous forms: monopoly, corporate, and global, reflecting technical and social development. The principles stated in the working-class definition are the same, but the actors may take different forms—proletarian, blue collar, white collar, pink collar, precariat, professionals, managers, and technicians versus individual owners, corporate CEOs, venture capitalists, finance capitalists, and so on.

Currently, there is much discussion about corporations, probably because of the one hundred largest economies in the world, fifty-one are corporations, and they are easier and more concrete targets than capitalism. Nearly everyone has some reason to dislike or distrust corporations—we've all been hurt by them as competitors, employees, investors, or consumers. Some groups focus their energy on corporate reform. Such an approach often forgets that corporations are an expression of capitalism. All the key difficulties that the corporate critics point out—authoritarianism, constant expansion, exploitation of the workforce, the exclusive focus on profits, and turning everything and everyone into a commodity—are found in capitalism. The working-class analysis argues that the problem is not merely corporations but the system they are embedded in—capitalism.

Capitalism from the Working-Class Perspective: A Summary

Class analysis recognizes capitalism as a historically developing system where society's material needs are satisfied primarily through exchange in the market. In that practice, the working class turns itself into a commodity by selling its labor power to the capitalist class that owns the factories, businesses, and corporations. These owners give the workers back a portion of the value they create through wages and use the rest, the surplus, to grow their holdings, for if they don't grow, competing owners will swallow them up. The major struggle is between the working class (including the "shrinking middle class," for they also work) and the capitalist class, and it is invisible for the reason that the wage system gives the illusion that employees are paid the full equivalent of the value they produce; therefore, they have no rights to the control and use of the surplus. Production is measured in a quantifiable form—money. Reproduction, nurturance, and the historic superexploitation of women and people of color and currently unpopular ethnic groups are ignored or used to weaken the workforce by pitting one part of the working class against another. So, by selling their labor power to the capitalists, employees become exploited robots, incapable of fulfilling themselves as social beings with inherent worth, while the capitalists gain wealth and power through the control of the surplus.

The goal of class analysis is to better understand the pitfalls of our current socioeconomy and to create a new system based on different, more humane values. This new arrangement would overcome the division within capitalism and create a classless society where everyone could fully realize himself or herself. By uncovering the invisible class struggle, we can have access to a new understanding of capitalism, and with this understanding, we can propose an alternative.

CHAPTER 2

A Working Definition of Class

Labor is prior to, and independent of, capital. Capital is only the fruit of labor, and could never have existed if labor had not first existed. Labor is superior to capital, and deserves much the higher consideration.

—Abraham Lincoln

Capital is dead labor, which, vampire-like, lives only by sucking living labor, and lives the more, the more labor it sucks.

—Karl Marx

Here are some questions for you: When you use the word "class" or think about class, what does it mean to you? Do you accept the idea of class? Alternatively, do you reject the idea of class and say, "We're all Americans," or "All people are created equal," and yet judge others by their incomes, the way they dress, where they live, their jobs, what they know?

Americans think a lot about group differences, but they, along with many of our social scientists and media pundits, do not generally think of the differences as class demarcations. When people are polled on their class self-identification, nearly all surveys state that the great majority of Americans think of themselves as middle class.

Judith Martin (Miss Manners) playfully said, "There are three social classes in America: upper-middle class, middle class, and lower-middle class." This characterization is often based on the questions asked in surveys. When individuals are given the choice of lower, middle, and upper class, most choose middle class, since few want to call themselves lower class. According to the National Opinion Research Center, when working class is one of the options, almost half of the respondents self-identify as working class.[1] Of course, most of these differences in self-definitions are based on individual, unsystematic standards. Let us see if we can get more clarity.

The Mainstream Definition of Class

The mainstream perspective defines class as a group that shares a common status depending upon their place in some kind of hierarchy. For example, if we choose wealth as the hierarchy, the richer you are, the higher your class.

Almost all of us would agree that having a higher status or class, however we view it, is a good thing, and the higher your status, the better chance you will have for a long and successful life.[2] Epidemiologist Michael Marmot demonstrated that how we stand in the social hierarchy is related to our chances of getting sick and how long we will live. For example, in the United States, those in the poorest households have almost four times the risk of death than in those of the richest. Low status leads to stress, forcing people into a continuous crisis mode, which, coupled with poorer food choices and reduced opportunities for medical intervention and healthy recreation, lead the way to heart disease. Our class or status is about our chance to live a good, full life.[3]

As we go through school and through life, lots of us are driven by questions like, how can I improve my status? Our focus on improving our individual lives is a reflection of the American worldview. After all, "rugged individualism" is part of our American ethos. We believe that our society is powerful, owing to the energy, intelligence, and inventiveness of individuals. This individualistic orientation is often expressed through statements like, "Anyone can make it in this country; all they have to do is get off their duffs, work, educate themselves, and use common sense."

In addition to individualism, we also believe in egalitarianism, the belief in fairness. Individualism and egalitarianism are competing values. This helps to explain some of the difficulties we have about class. On the one hand, we blame individuals for being poor, and on the other, we are uncomfortable seeing the inequalities in our society. Discomfort is also seen in individuals' unwillingness to discuss their incomes in public for fear that they will be judged. The anxiety we have about our personal wealth and our location in the social hierarchy makes dialogue about class difficult.

Most persons, when asked about the economy, answer by reflecting the conventional cultural views, with emphasis on how the public is differentiated by identifiable traits, such as having a high-paying job, owning a car or two, having a mortgage on a house, being able to go on vacation, owning the appropriate home entertainment devices, having medical insurance, being able to send their children to college, and so on. This mainstream perspective identifies class as being composed of individuals and families who are ranked similarly on several measurable criteria (income, jobs, ownership of objects—especially of cars and homes—education, neighborhood).

The Working-Class Definition of Class

The working-class definition for class looks at society from the perspective of the relationship between contending groups—workers and capitalists.[4]

Up until now, I have used the terms "status" and "class" interchangeably. However, for the purpose of the working-class definition of "class," I need to be more precise. "Status" is focused on prestige, while "class" is based on socioeconomic position. The mainstream definition of "class" conflates the two terms. From the working-class perspective, linking status with class obscures the attempt to understand the way society works for these reasons: (1) people who focus on differences in status are concerned with the effects of the economy, so they often fail to examine the actual causes of the status differences—other than mentioning individual motivation; and (2) status ignores the key distinction between the workers and the capitalists (that the workers own their own labor power [see the glossary] and must sell it to the capitalists who own the businesses and that this process is exploitative).

Rather than looking at wealth or lifestyles (status), a class analysis begins by examining how society organizes production to meet its needs. This requires a structural approach (focusing on the system). Discussions of status differences and their effects on individuals, while tempting, ignore a structural analysis. For example, focusing on the inspiring stories of employees who fought against the odds and improved their lives by getting an education and raising their status is a diversion. Although these stories may serve to give hope and buoy up some employees, they often ignore the underlying structural causes of dissatisfaction and alienation. Inspiring stories are inspiring because they are unusual. They support the status-quo perspective of the capitalist class while they contradict the evidence that makes the stories so unusual.[5] Members of the working class are rarely able to accomplish such an improvement, and today, there is even less social mobility than in the 1980s.[6] What a class analysis will demonstrate is that the major cause of the anguish for the working class is capitalism, which, as we saw earlier, transforms human relations into relations between things that then define the nature of our lives—it is a system that dehumanizes employees and turns them into robots for the company.

The issue between the contending groups (working class versus capitalist class) is best understood by moving away from the individualistic focus on accumulating wealth and status to studying how groups historically organize to satisfy their needs for food, shelter, and clothing.

The first societies were hunter-gatherers. These small bands[7] had no hierarchical divisions, no classes. Over thousands of years, humans learned better ways of producing food. Then, with the advent of agriculture about ten thousand years ago, bands and tribal groups were able to sustain themselves and develop a surplus. This surplus allowed the formation of subgroups that were free to focus on activities other than food production: craftwork, trading, healing, organizing, and fighting. Society became more complex. A division of labor and a hierarchy developed, and one group began to exploit another. The first expression of exploitation was in ancient society: of women by men; of slaves by slave owners; and later, in feudal society, of serfs by landowners. With the shift to capitalism, where workers exchanged their labor for wages given by the capitalist, it seemed that exploitation ended.

Under capitalism, for the first time, it was not possible to hold shares in another person's labor (as was possible under conditions of slavery and partly possible in feudalism). Instead, each individual owned his or her labor power and was theoretically free to sell it to the highest bidder. This theoretical freedom is illusory, since—under industrialism—the workforce did not own the tools required to produce what they needed in order to survive. Capitalists owned the factories, machinery, and raw materials. Workers could only get what they needed by selling the one thing they had that the capitalist needed—their labor power, their ability to work.

On the surface, this seems like a fair exchange. But the wages workers receive are less than the amount of wealth they create for the capitalist. It might be possible for a worker to produce enough to cover the cost of his or her wage in four hours out of an eight-hour day. Unfortunately, the capitalist doesn't let the worker go home. Workers are still forced to work an extra four hours (or more). This unpaid labor, called surplus labor, is the source of profits for the capitalist. To the worker, it appears that he or she is being paid for a full day's work. So the exploitation through wages that lies at the heart of capitalism is camouflaged as the picture of fairness. (In my work experience, this was the hardest truth to understand, for the training that I got all my life was that the wage system was natural, even though it seemed unfair.)

In capitalism's early stage, the masses, pushed out of farming, were packed into the cities, where they experienced a loss of personal connection. Later, in industrial assembly-line work, workers did not produce a complete commodity, giving them the impression that they did not produce anything at all. These developments separated workers from their products and did not allow them to see the relevance of their labor to society. This confusion about the value of their labor power led many into a state of hopelessness and passivity. Work became a necessary drudgery. Fulfillment was pursued outside of the workplace, eventually transformed into our current culture of consumerism, with its focus on mind-deadening diversions (leisure) or fulfillment through buying and accumulating things.

The working-class definition of class focuses on a different question: if our society is so rich, why are there so many poor? This question compels us to look at society from the perspective of contending groups in relation to one another. We will define class as "that grouping of individuals with a common position in the production process, in relation to another group." This definition is more useful, because by defining social classes in terms of how labor is turned into money and not on how much money is earned, it keeps our focus on how the system works and on the relationship of workers to the capitalists—the owners of the means of production.

The mainstream definition of classes as rich and poor, educated and not educated, and so on relies on unclear categories. (Who decides how rich and poor are defined? Who decides how much and what kind of schooling is an education?) The working-class definition depends more on how society functions than on how individuals are categorized. It recognizes that there is a dynamic, continually changing relationship between the contending groups.

For example, the two classes continuously adjust to one another as technology advances: at one point, the working class was primarily composed of physical laborers, but as technology progressed, the working class included skilled technicians and office workers. From the working-class perspective, society is a dynamic arrangement of interrelated parts, and merely naming or categorizing the parts fails to understand, analyze, or recognize the relationship between the parts. If you are trying to understand how an engine works, you cannot effectively explain it by laying the parts out on the workbench, naming them, and talking about their characteristics (weight, shape, size, etc.). You need to explain the relationship between fuel, air, pistons, spark, ignition, drive shaft, and so on.

If you want to understand capitalism from the working-class perspective, you need to understand the dynamic relationship between the working class, the capitalist class, property, production, consumption, profit, surplus value, unemployment, and accumulation (definitions are in the glossary).

In our working-class definition, we will primarily focus on the historic and dynamic relationship between the two major classes: the capitalist class and the working class (we will discuss the middle class, ruling class, excluded workers, and underclass later). One class—the capitalist class—owns the land, raw materials, factories, and tools; the other—the working class—owns their power to labor. Some in the working class may own (along with the bank) a home, car, or other commodities, but that kind of wealth provides them with no control over the work of others.

How Did Capitalism Arise?

The transition to capitalism took place in different ways, at different times, in different regions. There are varying historical renditions of how bankers, merchants, and industrialists displaced landowners as holders of social, political, and economic power and how peasants were turned into workers. To be a satisfying explanation, there needs to be an answer to the question, how did capitalism start? Accumulating capital means that there must be surplus value, and in order for surplus value to exist, there must be capitalist production—but in order to have production, there must be capital and labor power. This becomes a vicious circle, the only way out is assuming a starting point that Marx called "primitive accumulation."

> The discovery of gold and silver in America, the extirpation, enslavement and entombment in mines of the aboriginal population, the beginning of the conquest and looting of the East Indies, the turning of Africa into a warren for the commercial hunting of black-skins, signalized the rosy dawn of the era of capitalist production. These idyllic proceedings are the chief momenta of primitive accumulation.[8]

Some other examples expanded on Marx's explanation or focused elsewhere:
- The countryside in sixteenth-century England,[9] where feudal lords realized that they could get more money from sheep than the crops forcefully taken from their peasants. They began the enclosure movement (an early act of privatization), seizing the common lands where the rural population lived, causing thousands of peasants to starve, become beggars, or, eventually, wage workers hired by the newly formed capitalists in the cities.
- The influence of the trading centers of Venice and Flanders, which then drew in the countryside.[10] Some argue that the Netherlands was the first thoroughly capitalist country, with Amsterdam having the first stock exchange.
- The rise of slavery, where the profits of the "triangular trade" between Europe, Africa, and America provided the capital for the industrial development of Britain.[11]
- The importance of military investment, where the emerging

nation-states needed their agrarian fighters to become soldiers, the first modern wage workers, requiring new, larger industries to produce weapons, ships, cannons, guns, and so on.[12]

- The importance of the world system. In response to the feudal crisis of climate change, declining agricultural production, and declining economies, Europe moved toward the establishment of a new economic arrangement in order to secure continued economic growth.
- The new world economy, capitalism, differed from earlier systems, because it was not wholly included in a single country—it was international. The control of labor around the world required strong state power in Western Europe. The regions that fed the capitalism of Europe broke down into four different categories—core, semiperiphery, periphery, and external—which describe each region's relative position within the world economy.[13] The core (England, France, and Holland) was the advanced economies of Europe that benefited most; the semiperipheries were core regions in decline (Portugal and Spain) or peripheries on the ascent (Italy, southern Germany, and southern France). The periphery (European colonies in Africa, Asia, and Latin American) was an occupied area that used enslaved persons to send raw materials to the core areas; the externals were economies not involved with this arrangement (Russia).
- Women's labor is central to capitalism's success. "Women and children comprised a major share of the entire manufacturing labor force during the initial period of industrialization."[14] From 1750, manufacturers found ways to combine female labor, using the excuse of national welfare and commercial independence. In 1791, Alexander Hamilton wrote in his *Report on Manufactures*, that "women and children are rendered more useful, and the latter more early useful by

- manufacturing establishments than they would otherwise be."[15]
- Capitalism was not exclusive to Europe and America. In the late 1800s, China, India, and the Middle East were nearly equal in economic development with Europe. Capitalism is a product of world history, and for a brief period in history, it focused on Western Europe and later went on to transform the world.[16]
- Political economy transformed during the Middle Ages from feudalism to capitalism simultaneously with changes in religious thought. The Protestant Reformation, especially with the establishment of Calvinism, played a major role in these changes, since—unlike other Christian sects—it believed that individuals, especially those who were well-off materially, were considered to be the "elect" of God and had high moral character—a perfect temperament for capitalism.[17]

The working-class understanding focuses on three points provided by the above analyses: (1) commodity production, (2) the capitalist, and (3) the worker.

1. Commodity production—The commodity market has its roots in the trading of agricultural products. In medieval times, goods were produced for use, and surplus was sent to small local markets where traditional "buy low and sell high" conditions operated. But as society developed, people began to exchange goods and services for other goods and services. At this stage, these goods and services became "commodities" (objects offered for sale or exchange in a market). In the marketplace where commodities are sold, the "use value" (usefulness) was not helpful in facilitating their sale, but their "exchange value"—a value that could

be expressed in the market—created the newly forming economic logic of capitalism.

2. Capitalists—The earliest capitalists can be traced back to early forms of merchant capitalism practiced in Europe during the Middle Ages. The small group of merchants, large landowners, moneylenders, and independent artisans financed the newly emerging industries requiring larger sums of capital. They, in time, formed the capitalist class.

3. Workers—Capitalism depended on the availability of laborers, some of whom were peasants that capitalist farmers pushed off the village commons and forced to move to cities to survive. They became the proletariat, working in the factories of the budding Industrial Revolution.

4. Many of the peasants who were driven off the land eventually migrated to the cities and became the labor force for capitalism. In their conversion, it was important that they not be able to sustain themselves as they could as peasants, for they had to be dependent on the capitalists. The only way workers could survive in this arrangement was to sell their labor power. They would work for the owners so as to receive a wage for that work. With these wages, they could purchase what they needed for survival. Because of the difficulty of recruiting a sufficient labor force, women and children were often used. In the early nineteenth century, England had more than one million child workers, some as young as seven years old; they comprised 15 percent of the total labor force.[18] And, of course, in the colonies, slaves and indentured servants were used extensively.

The basic difference between precapitalist societies and capitalism is not whether production is urban or rural but about who owned what. The workers must have no ownership except over their own labor power, while the capitalists own almost everything else.

From this short historical excursion into the development of capitalism, we can point out the following: (1) capitalism is not "natural" but a human creation that arose at a certain time with a unique concurrence of historical circumstances; (2) capitalism contained a new economic logic, where virtually everything in society becomes a commodity produced for a market; (3) the assumption that humans bartered and exchanged in the market since the beginnings of history is not true, since production for the market was not the primary activity of precapitalist societies; and (4) under capitalism, society became a captive of the market, where persons were forced to organize themselves for work and to create commodities for exchange (to satisfy the market demands) and ultimately for profit rather than for use.

The development of capitalism demonstrates that the accumulation of capital needed to launch capitalism did not occur because a small group we now call capitalists were frugal and smart and saved their money or the group we now call the working class were lazy and stupid. It happened due to the forcible separation of the things necessary for people to produce with (land, tools, buildings, machines) from the possession of the workers and ownership being placed into the hands of the landowners and industrial leaders.

From the working-class perspective, there are two classes: one that has nothing but its labor power to sell, the working class; and the other that owns almost everything but needs employees to make it function, the capitalist class. In this relationship, the capitalist class had the advantage.

In slave society and under feudalism, the slaves and serfs were forced to produce goods and were given a portion for their upkeep while the owner or lord seized the surplus. What was produced was based on needs of the society and not on the requirement to make profit and accumulate more capital to invest.

In feudal society, the serfs had historical rights to some of the means of production (seeds, agricultural tools) and also had possession of the product of labor, mostly agricultural products, which the landlords had to take away, sometimes through force and other times through mutual agreement.

Under capitalism, since the capitalist class owns the means of production, it seizes the surplus that the workers produce above their wages. This surplus, known as surplus value, is also known as profit from the perspective of the capitalist and exploitation from the perspective of the workers. Thus, the workforce creates the surplus value but does not control its use.

In capitalism, the motive for producing goods and services is to sell them for a profit. This profit motive is a revolutionary change in economic logic. The focus on profit requires that resources be used for whatever provides the most profit (e.g., building tanks instead of public housing). Unprofitable needs are not invested in, despite their importance (e.g., rivers, lakes, and oceans won't be cleaned, and global warming, ocean acidification, and the collapse of biodiversity won't be addressed, since there is no profit in it; pharmaceutical companies aren't interested in research on easily available herbs for healing, as there is not enough profit in that research). This profit motive that places profit above human needs and the environment is the source of the largest part of the world's problems: starvation, war, crime, and environmental degradation.[19]

The profit motive is not merely an expression of greed. Capitalists do not have a choice about it, for the need to make a profit is imposed on them. The firm either grows or dies, as do the capitalists who own it. Competition with other capitalists forces them to reinvest as much of their profits as they can afford (while maintaining their lifestyles) to keep their production competitive. The profit motive allows for the creation of a society based on continual growth, and since the earth is finite, there must eventually be collapse or financial catastrophes, which include capitalism's periodic downturns: overproduction coupled with depressed wages and limited markets for goods (see appendix 2). Our oceans, forests, polar ice cap, fertile land, and atmosphere are now put at risk by the global growth of capitalism.[20]

The capitalist class maintains control of surplus value by keeping a significant portion of the working class disorganized, fighting with one another, deprived and fearful of losing what insufficient wages it has. It covers up this inequality through the use of its control of advertising, schools, media, government, religion, and so forth to promote its perspective. This barrage of propaganda gets the working class to shift its focus from the system to the individual, leaving a lot of workers believing that if you apply yourself, work hard, and study hard, you will be a success in America, and if you don't, it's your own fault.

The reason why the working class is poorer and less educated than the capitalist class is not due to individual motivation or lack of intelligence, skill, or luck but because it doesn't have access to the money and power to make a better life for itself and must depend on the "generosity" of the capitalist class.

This understanding of class from the perspective of the interrelationship of groups, production, and surplus value provides the tools that allow us to understand that the relationship between worker and owner is exploitative, involving a constant transfer of wealth from the workforce to the owners.

This working-class approach has certain advantages over the mainstream definition. It is founded on a defensible, articulated theory that explains how wealth and power is created in society. In addition, it helps explain the life conditions of the vast majority of people in the world.

This perspective has three problems:

1. It can get you in trouble. There is a good reason why politicians rail against those who point out the inequalities in our society and call them promoters of "class war"—this approach exposes the injustice of the status quo, and those in power do not tolerate that exposure lightly.
2. It can get you in trouble with yourself, for it requires some study and discipline that will cause you to question your

assumptions, develop a new way of thinking, and motivate you to ask different and perhaps uncomfortable questions.
3. Since it was developed in the nineteenth century, when class divisions were easier to distinguish, it can be criticized for not adequately addressing changes in our society. These are some examples: the emerging middle class, the separation of ownership from control, the appearance of corporations, the managerial revolution, financial capital, globalization, the role of women and minorities, as well as the changing dynamics of the information age.

Problem one cannot be solved: disagreement is part of the human condition, and you need to be prepared to communicate.[21] Problems two and three will be addressed in the following pages.

Summary

Mainstream perspective (not held in this book)
Definition of class: A class is composed of individuals and families who are ranked similarly on several criteria—income, occupation, power, and so forth.
Question: How can I improve my status?
Action: I work for money in order to buy things in order to be successful.
Focus: On status, the self, the market and commodities.
Solution: Work more and consume more.
Effect on society: Helps to maintain the status quo, increases wealth inequality, increases pollution as well as potential wars over declining natural resources.

Working class perspective (held in this book)
Definition: A class is that grouping of individuals with a common position in the production process, in relation to another group.
Question: If our society is so rich, why are there so many poor?

Action: Begin by understanding the production process to find where wealth is siphoned off from the workers to the owners.
Focus: On the group and production.
Solution: Workers first take charge of surplus value (labor for which workers are not paid) and use it for the whole of society. Create a classless society that does not depend on surplus value. (Easier said than done.)
Effect on society: Critical of status quo.

Definitions Have Consequences

> It's not easy to contribute our middle-class skills and ideas without dominating. It's not easy to find a balance between over-emphasizing middle-class worldviews and over-relying on other people's thinking just because they are working-class. We find the balance when we listen more to working-class people and to our own best judgment as well.
> —Betsy Leondar-Wright[22]

> In general, in a deep conflict, the eyes of the downtrodden are more acute about the reality of the present. For it is in their interest to perceive correctly in order to expose the hypocrisies of the rulers. They have less interest in ideological deflection.
> —Immanuel Wallerstein

I have presented you with two of the major definitions of class: the mainstream and the working class. The mainstream perspective defines class as a group of individuals who share a common status depending upon where they are placed on a hierarchy that may include income, wealth, education, and so on. This perspective focuses on the effects of the social arrangement on the winners and losers. In the mainstream perspective, classes are generally divided into three groups: working class, middle class, and upper class, although some theorists make finer distinctions, such as lower working class, upper working class, lower middle class, upper middle class, lower upper class, and so on.

The working-class perspective defines class as a group that is determined by their relationship to the material/economic resources (the means of production)—the capitalist class owns them, and the working class works them but does not own them. This two-class perspective focuses on the system, which explains how wealth and profit are produced, controlled, and distributed.

Social activists who use the mainstream model are not so concerned with the dynamics of capitalism but with solving specific problems that occur because of status inequality: excessive poverty, lack of health care, poor schooling, access to jobs, and so on. They try to solve social problems by improving equality through legislative action, political pressure, education, empowerment training, social action, psychological techniques, and the like.

Social activists who use the working-class model focus on the structure that causes the unfairness. This group argues that capitalism is unjust and unfair due to a design flaw, the necessity of a class system that fails to give the vast majority fulfilling lives. These activists work on organizing the working class through action and education, with the final purpose of changing the structure and eradicating the necessity for classes.

Mainstream social activists, who often define themselves as being "middle class,"[23] prefer their approach, since it seems effective and not excessively disruptive of the status quo. They inadvertently accept capitalism by focusing their energy on improving it through raising the status of low-standing individuals and groups. This mainstream approach has undeniably introduced improvements to our society, and countless individuals have better lives because of it. For example, we have shorter hours at work, overtime pay, weekends off, better health care, food stamps, welfare rights, and so on. However, it functions like a social Band-Aid. When a problem arises, social activists organize to solve it. And like a Band-Aid, the solution only deals with the effect, which means that the same problem will probably reoccur at a later time (for example, even though unions heroically fought for reduced working hours and so on, we are now facing increases in working hours and working days, and fewer employees, the loss of much overtime pay, the reduction of health care, the loss of retirements, the loss of welfare rights, and the growth of unemployment, and the like).

In addition, as Betsy Leondar-Wright stated above, lots of the mainstream activists who are "middle class" often don't listen to the workers, since they have their own agendas and think they know better about what the workers need than the workers themselves.[24] An instructive story attributed to Linda Stout,[25] an activist for the working class, was about a group of workers who were putting a brochure together that stated "something has got to be wrong when the government spends so much money on the military and nothing on me!" A well-meaning middle-class editor changed that phrase to "I don't understand why the government spends so much money on the military and nothing on me." Such a change made the original writers angry, who stated, "What do you mean we don't understand? Of course we understand! Do you think we're stupid or something?" Working classes know they are being exploited; they don't need to be told about their condition by relatively comfortable activists. They do, however, need a systematic understanding about how capitalism works—they need to develop a class analysis.

The working-class perspective sees capitalism as its enemy. It is concerned primarily with the question, if capitalism hurts most people, why keep it? Social activists for the working class know that most workers understand they are being hurt by the system since they talk to, identify with, and listen to one another. They approach problems by teaching class analysis through

1. organizing based on the awareness that the working class

has of being exploited; going to the working class in their neighborhoods, homes, churches, and meeting places;
2. contradicting the capitalist propaganda about the meaning of democracy,[26] equal opportunity, and climbing the ladder of success;
3. focusing on winning—not merely celebrating—the good fight; there have been too many marches and reactions against oppression that ended when all the middle-class social activists went home patting themselves on the back with no follow-through; and
4. providing an alternative vision to the current system as well as a path to reaching it, while at the same time pointing out how capitalism is destructive by turning humans into things, alienated robots, or zombies.[27]

The middle-class approach, in its attempt to help the downtrodden, ultimately supports happier consumers, whose consuming habits support the growth and strength of the system. The working-class approach struggles against the domination of capitalism. There needs to be a middle ground that works to reform inequities while at the same time organizes to eventually overturn and replace capitalism.

CHAPTER 3

What Is Class Analysis?

In general, the art of government consists of taking as much money as possible from one class of citizens to give to another.

—Voltaire

Ask anyone committed to Marxist analysis how many angels on the head of a pin, and you will be asked in return to never mind the angels, tell me who controls the production of pins.

—Joan Didion

What is class analysis? It is a way of thinking which recognizes that our society is composed of classes and that lots of our thoughts and actions are filtered through that awareness. Studying class means studying a group in terms of its relation to the way society produces its material wealth. Class analysis recognizes that the foundation of any society is its productive relations and matching class relations. This perspective is in contrast to numerous ways of examining and describing society in terms of individuals, family, religion, political parties, language, race, gender, status, and so on.

Class analysis, as described in this book, recognizes that struggles like racism and sexism must also be addressed, for all oppression is contrary to the goal of class analysis— that is, to create a classless society. As long as there is wage labor (exploitation) that leads to class oppression (where one class has the power to dominate another class), there will be racial oppression and sexism. Class analysis doesn't wish to separate exploitation from oppression (see glossary); it seeks to show how they are connected. The capitalist class uses the divisions between groups found in racism and sexism to weaken the bonds between workers in order to manipulate and control them.

Class analysis is rarely used to evaluate and solve problems in our society. For example, if we're trying to figure out how to improve our schools, we can propose different curricula, new methods of evaluating students and teachers, new ways of increasing attendance, developing multicultural or gender-sensitive programs, longer school hours, merit-based pay for teachers, smaller classrooms, more computers, better training for teachers, zero tolerance, and so on. It is rare that we consider class. Some educators do investigate the possibility that "middle-class" (explained below) and "working-class" students are treated unequally, with different goals, values, and learning styles.[1] But this is not enough, as that type of explanation usually employs the mainstream definition of class that is based on status, on the effects of class divisions, and not on the cause. Class analysis, as defined here, concentrates on explaining the causes of inequality, for the roots of human oppression and alienation lie in the very way that society itself is organized. By ignoring social class, the causes of inequality are unseen.[2]

Jean Anyon, an education researcher pointed out that schools in rich communities were much better than those in poor communities and prepared their students for good jobs. In her research she found, as did earlier educational scholars, that

> students in different social-class backgrounds are rewarded for classroom behaviors that correspond to personality traits allegedly rewarded in the different occupational strata--the working classes for docility

and obedience, the managerial classes for initiative and personal assertiveness. Basil Bernstein, Pierre Bourdieu, and Michael W. Apple focusing on school knowledge, have argued that knowledge and skills leading to social power and regard (medical, legal, managerial) are made available to the advantaged social groups but are withheld from the working classes to whom a more "practical" curriculum is offered (manual skills, clerical knowledge).[3]

Evaluations of the educational structure that do not recognize that our society is class based will inevitably propose superficial solutions. A mainstream inquiry will try to solve the crisis in education by looking at the effects and solve those effects by blaming teachers and requiring better teacher training and testing programs like No Child Left Behind, Race to the Top, vouchers, and privatization. In contrast to the "effects" approach, a class analysis will look at the underlying cause—the system: unemployment, poverty, immigration, racism, shattered neighborhoods, the hopelessness of the lives of most working-class families and inner-city communities—and work to solve those problems. A good example of such a solution can be found in the high-performing schools of Finland, where the students are provided with food, free health care, and developmental needs and counseling services that are regularly available.

Why Class Analysis Is Important

A hundred times every day I remind myself that my inner and outer life depend on the labors of other men, living and dead, and that I must exert myself in order to give in the same measure as I have received and am still receiving.

Albert Einstein

| *Gus Bagakis* |

There is nobody in this country who got rich on his own. Nobody.

—Elizabeth Warren

Class analysis is important. It gives us a way to understand how our society functions, how profit is made, why there are rich and poor, powerful and vulnerable, and why some are paid attention to while most are ignored. On a personal level, a class analysis can help explain whom we marry, what health care we have, how much respect or disrespect we are given, and how long and how well we will live.

Class analysis focuses on the activity that most of us do for most of our lives—work. When humans lived in bands and tribes, material goods were valued, since they maintained the group: individuals worked to live (work supplied them with their needs). In class society, dominant ruling classes—like those in ancient slavery and feudalism—forced people to work for them. This "forcing" was transformed into wage labor under capitalism. In this new society, our society, almost all of our life is organized around the work of producing products (commodities) for the market. In our society, individuals live to work (they define themselves through their work).

Individuals who are not unemployed are working more and more hours throughout the year. To stay ahead, they are expected to go to work earlier and stay later. The normal eight-hour workday is no longer good enough: "the average person is now on the job an additional 163 hours, or the equivalent of an extra month a year." [4]

According to the International Labor Organization, Americans now work 1,978 hours annually. The average American worked 199 hours more in 2000 than he or she did in 1973.[5] Our commutes are increasingly difficult, our jobs are less stable, and our pay is shrinking, so more family members must work. Our benefits are disappearing, our housing is more expensive, and our leisure time is vanishing.[6] This condition of "time poverty," the stealing of time from workers, further destroys the quality of their lives.[7] In addition, the United States is the only advanced industrial country without a national paid parental leave benefit and universal health care.

Since we live in a society where the majority of our lifetime is organized around work (educating ourselves for it, going to it, doing it [or not if you're unemployed], gaining our identity from it [or not], retiring from it, or dying because of it), we need a conceptual tool to help us understand it. Class analysis can be that tool, for it opens an important window into our society. However, in order to conduct class analysis, we need to learn to think in a different way.

Studying Class: Groups, Not Individuals

Society does not consist of individuals but expresses the sum of interrelations, the relations within which these individuals stand.

—Karl Marx

A class is a group of human beings who share common interests because they experience common conditions. In class analysis, the terms we use—like "capitalist class"—should not necessarily lead to judgments or criticisms of individuals within these classes. Classes do, however, reveal the limitations and opportunities for individuals within each class. I propose to focus more on the effects of class membership on individuals rather than on blaming individuals for their actions. For example, a corporate board chairman born into a wealthy family can be a compassionate individual, a philanthropist, and a devoted father and husband. At the same time, the nature of his life experience as a member of the capitalist class forces him to act in a certain way that is beneficial to his class. He can lay off a group of employees or shut down a factory. These actions, which are catastrophic to the lives of the working class, are based on the need for his corporation to survive in the competitive market and not on his personality or character. It is true that as a member of the capitalist class, he is responsible for the workers' catastrophe, but focusing our blame on the individual obscures an understanding of how capitalism creates an unequal society and extracts profits from the employees by paying them less than the value they created through their work.

Production: The Heart of Class Analysis

As I pass up and down [my city's] streets I see in many places the work my own hands have wrought on her buildings and I feel that in a sense I am a part of our city. My strength and whatever skills I possess are woven into her material fabric that will remain when I am gone, for Labor is Life taking a permanent form.
—Walter Stevenson, union carpenter, 1930

Woman has been the great unpaid laborer of the world.[8]
—Elizabeth Cady Stanton, Susan Brownell Anthony, Matilda Joslyn Gage, Ida Husted

It may seem peculiar that the working-class definition of class focuses on production, since consumer culture is currently central to our lives. It is not because consumption is not important; in fact, the reason (given by capitalists) for production is consumption (even though the real reason for production is profit, since commodities are primarily produced for exchange, not necessarily for use).

Currently, consumers are spoken of as if they were a separate group with separate interests from producers. The shift toward a focus on consumerism occurred largely because, in complex modern industrial societies, consumption and production have become separated. Commodities began to act as the driving force for the economy, due to the mass production methods similar to those initiated by Ford in the beginning of the twentieth century, when businesses needed to sell more and more commodities so that they could derive more profits while competing with other firms. It's either sell or die. This led to the development of the advertising industry that pushed consumption to create and fulfill the dreams of alienated workers. Advertising stimulated workers' fantasies by convincing them that products would make them happy, when much of the time their effect was to increase desires and keep employees trapped. The effects of consumerism depoliticized workers and got them to think like consumers rather than like citizens.

By recognizing the significance of production and the production process, a class analysis brings back an important dimension to our understanding. We can see, on the shop floor and in the corporate cubicle, for example, how employees are isolated, manipulated, and disrespected, how surplus value is extracted, and how the capitalist class expropriates profit from them while at the same time controlling them.

Some feminists correctly argue that focusing on production too often leaves little recognition of the reproduction of the labor force, the nurturing dimension that has been historically relegated to women (see "What about Gender and Race?" in chapter 6). The two quotes that began this section may lead you to ask Walter Stevenson (quoted above) how he was able to maintain and develop his strength and skills. The answer was probably through the nurturance provided by the unpaid labor of Mrs. Stevenson.

By looking at consumption through the production process, we can see that lots of the things we purchase are intended to fill a feeling of emptiness, since this class-based system separates us from one another, from our environment, and from ourselves. How many things do you own that you purchased to satisfy some unspecified need, and now that you have them, you realize that the need has not been satisfied? So out you go to purchase new things. Needs are in part produced due to the creation of a state of alienation and unhappiness, an outgrowth of the restrictions placed on workers in the production process.[9]

What do workers need? They need loving relationships, shelter, clothing, food, health, a chance to create, to be challenged, a relationship with nature, and acknowledgment by their community. Most of these needs can be satisfied outside of our shopping centers.

This focus on production is related to a particular conception of human nature. Human beings are defined in various ways: as rational beings, social animals, creations of God, thinking substances, exceptional primates, fundamentally good, and so on. The production view sees labor as the central distinction between human beings and other species. Through the tool in the form of a weapon, human society became possible. Weapons became equalizers, and as soon as all males were armed, the cost of monopolizing a large number of females was lessened: no more alpha males could run the society, as did other primates. The protohumanoids became polygynous (having more than one wife at a time), leading to general polygyny, and finally to monogamy as well as a more cooperative larger society.[10] Although animals labor in the world, what distinguishes humans from other animals is that, for humans, labor is a conscious activity. Animals behave in the world while humans consciously act upon it. (Some recent findings by anthropologists question the finality of this distinction but still hold on to the importance of labor for human development)[11]. The anthropologist Eleanor Leacock stated,

> it was through labor that humanity created itself as a skillful, large-brained, language-using animal, and through labor that it created an elaborate cultural superstructure. The very impressiveness of mankind's mental achievements, however, has obscured the fundamental significance of labor. Furthermore, the separation of planning for labor from the labor itself, a development of complex society, contributed to the rise of an idealistic world

outlook, one that explains peoples' actions as arising out of thoughts instead of their needs.[12]

Production is central to our understanding of capitalism. On the one hand, it is through production (labor and creativity) that humans define and fulfill themselves. On the other hand, production in capitalism, with its oppressive class divisions, suffocates the humanity of the vast majority of workers.

CHAPTER 4

The Question about the Middle Class

We of the sinking middle class may sink without further struggles into the working class where we belong, and probably when we get there it will not be so dreadful as we feared, for, after all, we have nothing to lose.
—George Orwell

The mainstream perspective defines the middle class as that group whose income generally falls between the capitalist class and the working class.[1] It gets most of the attention from the media and from popular culture. Instead of calling the in-between group "middle class," we will call them "coordinators."[2] Why? There are two major reasons: (1) "middle class" is a cultural misunderstanding (explained below); and (2) even though coordinators are better educated, more highly skilled, or professionals, they are workers. They belong to the same class as other workers, since they too are given partial pay for the value they create or help create for the capitalist class. And in this text, the purpose of a class analysis is to focus on the structure of the social order: to demonstrate how profits are made and how the capitalists gain at the expense of the workforce.

Of course, a change in terms doesn't take away the anger that the working class has toward its immediate bosses or other members of the coordinator group (popularly known as the "middle class"), even if the anger is kept within the family. But the anger doesn't change the fact that the coordinators work for salaries or wages and that their objectives are to coordinate: to control, manage, and support the rest of the working class in order to facilitate the extraction of surplus value for the capitalist class.

Coordinators normally control workers, while workers commonly operate machines or do manual labor. Coordinators are divided into numerous subgroups: from supervisors on the job to well-paid upper management. Those who work closely with the ruling capitalist class generally hold the values and goals of the capitalist class. Even though the great majority of coordinators are closer in income and power to the traditional working class, they are not likely to identify with the working class due to the power of the capitalist-class message that success is related to status. So this group is more likely to maintain the status quo since they have mortgages and children in college and are generally better off than the rest of the workforce.

An analogy from our slave history demonstrates the relationship between the coordinators and the working class—the similarities and differences between house slaves and field slaves. House slaves, who were closer and who often had personal relationships with the master, had certain benefits, including being better fed and clothed than the field slaves. They received secondhand clothing from the master's family. In addition, house slaves were not as easily replaceable due to their training. Although house slaves often felt superior to field slaves (as managers often feel superior to workers), the fact remained that both groups were slaves—both were dependent on the power and whims of the master. Fortunately for the master, each group often disliked the other. Thus their potential power to unify and to overturn the master was significantly weakened.

Today, coordinators (house slaves) and the working class (field slaves) are creators of surplus value (see the glossary), and the capitalist class exploits them both. However, as in the house/field separation between slaves, those who receive better rewards—in this case, the coordinators—tend to align with the capitalist class. The result is that each segment of the working class distrusts the other. This distrust benefits the capitalist class—as it did the master in slave society.

The coordinators are frequently the bureaucrats who keep the structure running. When they misidentify as being middle class and not coordinators, they function as neutral, compliant cogs that identify with the corporations they work for. They then inadvertently enter the class war on the side of the ruling class. So the supposedly neutral term "middle class" becomes a cloak for ruling-class collaborators. These coordinators

> assure themselves of their own goodness through their private acts as husbands, wives, mothers and fathers. They sit on school boards. They go to Rotary. They attend church. It is moral schizophrenia. They erect walls to create an isolated consciousness. They make the lethal goals of Exxon Mobil or Goldman Sachs or Raytheon or insurance companies possible. They destroy the ecosystem, the economy and the body politic and turn workingmen and -women into impoverished serfs. They feel nothing ... Little acts of kindness and charity mask the monstrous evil they abet. And the system rolls forward. The polar ice caps melt. The droughts rage over cropland. The drones deliver death from the sky. The state moves inexorably forward to place us in chains. The sick die. The poor starve. The prisons fill. And the careerist, plodding forward, does his or her job.[3]

There is some good news, though. The recent Occupy Wall Street and its offspring, the 99 Percent movement, which targets the 1 percent as the problem, can lead to a new sense of national identity not based on the myth that we are middle class but on the reality that we are divided between the rulers and the ruled, the rich and the poor, the powerful and the weak—that we are a class-divided nation.

Why Is It Hard to Drop the Concept "Middle Class"?

> *If the worker and his boss enjoy the same television program and visit the same resort places, if the typist is attractively made up as the daughter of her employer, if the Negro owns a Cadillac, if they all read the same newspaper, then this assimilation indicates not the disappearance of classes, but the extent to which the needs and satisfactions that serve the preservation of the establishment are shared by the underlying population.*
>
> —Herbert Marcuse, 1964

Why does the concept "middle class" persist? There are lots of reasons, in addition to the ones cited by Marcuse above, for the promotion of "middle class" and the conscious suppression of "working class" in our society.

1. The origins of the America theory—Early European immigrants escaped the restrictions and limitations of being branded as "the working class" in their countries of origin in order to find freedom and the possibility of a good life in America. And that good life meant the possibility of moving up from the working class to the middle class.
2. The code-word theory—In the eighteenth century, "middle class" was a term that separated the yeoman farmers from the poor and the nonwhites.[4] "Middle class" has become a code word for white people, maintaining the white status quo. ("Black middle class" is used to indicate African American newcomers to a level of economic or educational advancement.)

3. The Horatio Alger theory (a nineteenth-century American author who wrote about young boys succeeding in America through hard work and deserved luck)—The few who are able to rise above their restricted class origins are celebrated, giving the illusion that our society allows for massive mobility to the middle class.
4. The promotion of consumerism—The purpose of advertisements is to tell us who we are through our possession of commodities, and the media promotes the lifestyle of the "middle class," for they have the income that advertisers want and keep the economy running.
5. The communist scare—The recollection of the red scare, the communist workers' state embodied in the Soviet Union, encourages the replacement of the term "workers" with the less dangerous term "middle class." In addition, the fear of workers is related to the historic distrust of unions by our business sector, government, and mass media.
6. What the mass media promote—Since the capitalist class owns the mass media, there is biased coverage of class issues, where the middle class is assumed to be the norm. There is no labor page in the newspaper. There is a business section, and any discussion about labor is relegated to a subsection of the business section or to negative depictions of violent workers on strike.
7. The goals of higher education—The persistence of attaining the dream of being middle class are encouraged in most universities. School curricula also support the middle-class worldview that encourages competition for external rewards, prioritizing mental over manual labor, and the pursuit of upward mobility through following the rules of the institution, all this while primarily focusing on the individual over the community.
8. The maintenance of the status quo—The opinion makers consider the promotion of "middle class" as a force for

stability and democracy and the taming of the potential threat to the social order by the "working class."
9. The American dream theory—The "middle class" is the entrance to the dream of consumerism: a house, a car, a good education, leisure time, and so on.

Words are powerful, since they influence our understanding of the world. When "middle class" replaces "working class," the capitalist class becomes less visible as the clear contrast between workers and bosses/owners disappears. The capitalist class, even when it is visible, is seen as the rich, a small group on top of the economic ladder, who is smarter, more talented, or more motivated than the rest of us. The image of the ladder supports the status quo by demonstrating that the path to success is the willingness and capacity of the individual to move up the ladder. In this model, most of us are in the middle of the ladder—those at the top of the ladder are seen as being unusually talented, and those at the bottom are thought of as employees with limited skills and motivation.

Many studies demonstrate reasons for the lack of upward mobility of the workforce.[5] In addition, workers have been taught to blame themselves for their inability to rise up the ladder, or they came to believe that they were on their way up the ladder after they improved their skills or attitudes. In focusing on this latter dynamic, John Steinbeck pointed out that workers often didn't see themselves as exploited proletariat (nineteenth-century term for workers) but as temporarily embarrassed millionaires.[6]

How often have you used a ladder and looked over to the person next to you? I would venture to say never, for they are either above or below you on the ladder, or you are on it alone. The ladder metaphor takes the focus away from the group and places it on to the individual perched on the ladder. This individualistic approach argues that individuals seeking their interests will create and maintain a healthy society. This method forgets that individuals are social beings and that our society is also composed of groups—organizations, assemblies, and communities—and it is through these groups that individuals often find their strength.

The capitalist class supports individualism, because individuals who think of themselves as isolated atoms tend not to organize and change the status quo. While it spreads this individualistic view publicly, the capitalist class privately recognizes that groups actually develop and maintain society. The government is composed of and controlled by groups (corporations or industries) represented by thousands of lobbyists who determine much of what is legislated.[7]

The individualistic perspective looks to the effects of society on individuals. It has little concern or awareness of the underlying structure that makes society a unified whole. When we complain about problems on the highway, we usually attribute the problem to gridlock, traffic jams, and road rage. We rarely look at the underlying conditions: the speeding up of our economy related to the speeding up of capital accumulation (the diversion of profits for the speeding up of growth, necessary for maintaining capitalism), the increasing shift toward the urbanization or suburbanization of our society related to the needs of businesses, or even the allocation of funds for roads and public transportation, depending on the pressures on the legislature by business interests. The individualistic perspective rarely looks at who's running the show—the capitalist class.

An extreme example of the inability to look at the underlying structure is the old joke about a driver, low on fuel, who entered a service station for some gas and said to the attendant, "It is amazing to me how you folks have been able to open gas stations directly over gas deposits in the earth and be so accurate about it!" This unbelievable customer would have no idea about the political power of the petroleum industry or of how petroleum is found, refined, transported, and stored in tanks under the station—that is, have no idea of the underlying structure providing him or her with gas.

| *Seeing Through The System* |

How Do "Coordinators" Differ from the Working Class?

The middle class [coordinators] insists on interpreting everyone else's reality through their own lens, for they believe their worldview is the only worldview.

—Anonymous

Although coordinators and workers are part of the working class, some significant traits differentiate these two subgroups of the working class. In my experience, these differences can often be seen in community meetings or church groups where members are able to select their tasks. I have seen numerous instances where the coordinators did the talking and leading, while we, the members of the traditional working class, arranged the chairs and cleaned up. I experienced this intraclass divide most powerfully in consciousness-raising organizations whose task was to promote the liberation of some oppressed group. In our group work, we all reverted to our traditional subgroups—the working class did the physical work while the coordinators did the organizing and planning. If you find yourself in a situation where the two groups are working together, notice who does the physical work and who does the mental work.

Of course, in most cases, coordinators and workers will not have contact with one another in a neighborhood setting due to differences in their wealth, education, and status. The point of contact between them is usually on the job, where the coordinators usually focus on mental work, while the workers focus on physical work.

This dynamic can be seen when working-class friends find out about my job as a philosophy instructor. They are often intimidated. They usually think of philosophy as the study of abstract ideas that are irrelevant to their lives or a complexity that is beyond their minds. In fact, one of the reasons I studied philosophy was due to my working-class anger at being excluded from the intellectual world practiced by the coordinators. I thought I would show "the man" that I could play his game. Even in the early days of Greek philosophy, the locals made fun of Thales, who is often cited as the first Western philosopher. The peasants retold a story of him walking along, looking up at the stars, and falling into a ditch. From the perspective of the peasants, he was off in his abstract world, not paying attention to his surroundings.

This story captures one difference between coordinator and working-class perspectives on thinking and ideas. The working-class perspective recognizes a close relationship between thinking and action. Concepts are tools that are used to describe and solve problems in the material world. The coordinators' "in-between" position in society often leaves them confused about where they stand (with the working class or with the owning class). In order to overcome their confusion, the coordinators rely on thinking and ideas (mental labor) to create their place in society.

The coordinators need to recognize[8] how they have been hurt by the advantages of wealth, security, and comfort. This seems difficult to do, but it is possible, since more and more coordinators recognize that their advantages are empty of content. Coordinators have no family time or leisure, as everyone is busy trying to make money, and they have the constant fear of losing hard-won advantages by being caught in downsizing or restructuring at work.[9] They conduct daily life in a background of growing insecurity with no compensating community support. The increasing social isolation and alienation in coordinators' lives takes away the sense of meaning and belonging that a community provides.

By integrating with the working class, the coordinators will learn the importance of the group. Coordinators will gain a new sense of identity and solidarity consistent with the social nature of human beings. Many coordinators may come to see that we are all in it together, and they will experience the exhilaration of the transition from "I" to "we." This experience often takes place after disasters, hurricanes, earthquakes, floods, and so forth, where we come together to help one another. We need to learn its benefits in everyday situations too.

This may all seem like pie in the sky, but as capitalism continues its damage of the earth and increases the separation of the classes, where the rich are getting richer and the poor are getting poorer, more of those in the middle will end up with the poor.[10] In a recent University of California study, it was found that fourteen million white-collar jobs are vulnerable to being outsourced.[11] These are jobs that include information technology, accounting, architecture, engineering design, news reporting, stock analysis, and medical and legal services.[12]

It is amazing how a change can transform the consciousness of the coordinators. Even medical doctors can change. In June 1999, doctors voted to form a labor union. They did so because Dr. Thomas Reardon, the head of the AMA, stated, "The physicians feel very frustrated, very disenfranchised, very helpless individually dealing with large managed care organizations and dealing with patient care issues. Now, what we need is a collective voice to begin to represent our patients."[13] If Dr. Reardon understood class analysis, he may have pointed out that the capitalist class was continually looking for ways to increase capital accumulation in its constant need to compete with other capitalist concerns, to either grow or die. And the introduction of managed care was one step in that process, while the doctors' reaction was to organize and fight for a larger cut of the profits.

The mental labor of doctors and most coordinators is made possible due to centuries of labor done by the slaves, serfs, and workers who have created the conditions and leisure to allow certain members of their communities to think and reflect. I am able to study and write, thanks to my working-class father, who worked as a coal miner and fruit peddler to bring up his children to be educated, as well as my mother, who not only was a homemaker but also worked at the canneries in the summer. I sit on a chair made by a laborer. I study in a library built by labor. The foods I eat, the clothing I wear, the transportation I use, the streets I walk on, and my shelter are all products of labor.

Part of the working-class distrust of abstract thought is based on the internalization by the working class of the lie perpetrated by this society that they are stupid and cannot learn. The country bumpkin, the hillbilly, the redneck, the beer-bellied factory worker, and those with a rural/Southern accent are all characteristics equated with stupidity. This is the stereotype of the working class, but there is abundant evidence of their brilliance.[14] A good example can be seen in the thinking process of an auto mechanic who diagnoses an automobile electrical problem, the method a maid or janitor uses to efficiently clean a house without exhausting themselves before they finish the job, or even the approach that a cook and waitress in the local diner have to the rapid growth of customers after a local theater lets out. Yet though the working class built the world we occupy and provides us with the items we need for survival, this stereotype prevails.[15]

Another example of the brilliance of the working class is demonstrated in a book titled *A People's History of Science: Miners, Midwives, and "Low Mechanicks"* by Clifford D. Conner. It points out that the traditional history of science that relies on individual geniuses like Galileo, Newton, Darwin, or Einstein is incomplete, since the contributions of workers and peasants have been ignored. Conner presented evidence like that of Onesimus, an African slave who showed how to prevent smallpox to North America early in the eighteenth century, a major contribution to the science of epidemiology. This was the outcome of the experimentation of thousands of his African lineage, whose names are lost in history. The book is full of examples like this.

The working class must develop its own thinkers, and the coordinators must actively ally with their fellow workers. Together, they can recognize their similar relation to the capitalist class, unify, and in turn overthrow the control and exclusive ownership of the ruling capitalist class, hopefully with some compassionate ruling-class allies, and create a classless society.

The relationship between the coordinators and the working class is similar to a relationship described in Aristophanes's story in Plato's *Symposium*. Aristophanes described magnificent four-armed and four-footed round beings, with heads with two faces and so forth, who were rivals to the gods. As punishment for their rebellion, Zeus, the head of the gods, split them in two, weakening them by creating the males and females of the human race. From that time on, women and men spent their lives searching for their other halves.

Class history is reminiscent of Aristophanes's fable. At an earlier time, human society was composed of tribal groups, where the only hierarchy was based on individual talent that directly benefited the whole community. For the most part, people were communal beings, supporting one another. With the development of agriculture and the division of labor, the creation of surplus goods and private property, classes came into being. Before the breakdown of society into classes, the division of labor was primarily based on kinship relations, age, sex, and position within the tribal group. With the ending of tribal society and the formation of classes, a new kind of division of labor began that was based on class relations, including the division between mental and manual labor, between managers (coordinators) and laborers, controlled and manipulated by the new gods. The new gods—the priests, kings, political leaders, landowners, capitalists, multinational and transnational corporations—also attacked any movement by workers trying to reproduce the earlier unity of the less alienated and powerful tribal communities—for example, workers forming unions or collectives to protect and develop themselves.[16]

These new "gods" held on to their power by turning groups against one another with various divisive schemes: excessive individualism, racism, anti-Semitism, sexism, adultism, ageism, ethnocentrism, patriotism, and so forth. While the earlier myth describes men and women seeking one another for completion, the working class and coordinators must seek one another to create a just society and dethrone the "gods." After overthrowing the gods, a new society must be created by the working class as a whole and not merely the coordinator subsection, too many of whom consciously or unconsciously hold on to the values and worldviews of the former gods, the capitalists.

CHAPTER 5
The Ruling Class

If the worker who produces wealth is not entitled to it, who is?
— Eugene V. Debs

All for ourselves and nothing for other people, seems, in every age of the world, to have been the vile maxim of the masters of mankind.
— Adam Smith

Everybody knows that the dice are loaded
Everybody rolls with their fingers crossed ...
Everybody knows the fight was fixed
The poor stay poor, the rich get rich
— Leonard Cohen

Working people know that "the dice are loaded" and "you can't fight city hall," but they haven't spent much time figuring out who has the money and power, how they get it, and how they keep it. After all, how could they? They're too busy trying to survive while at the same time being bombarded with the ruling-class message that their powerlessness and poverty are their own faults.

The class analysis approach argues that a small group of capitalists,

| *Seeing Through The System* |

the ruling class,[1] holds the greatest concentration of wealth and power in the US political economy and chooses to actively set the agenda that the country will follow.[2] It controls the manufacturing, the finances, the political sphere, the courts, the military, the police, the schools, and the methods of persuasion.

In his book *Who Rules America?*,[3] William Domhoff pointed out that the idea that a small ruling class runs America puts most persons off. Why? People believe what they've been trained to believe, that they are in control of their lives since they live in a democracy. Additional reasons for not accepting the possibility of the existence of a ruling class are these: (1) the concept of class is not generally accepted, (2) some believe that the increased complexity of society means that power is not held by one group but is divided among groups whose interests are different, and (3) the ruling class uses its power and control of media to hide its existence.

1. The hidden existence of class was discussed in chapter 1, which explained that class disappeared from public awareness and that almost everyone believed that they were part of one big middle class. The use of "middle class" corrupted the meaning of class as a contentious term designating the struggle between the working class and the capitalist class.
2. The "complexity of society" argument doesn't account for the fact that a small group has the wealth and power in our society:[4]
    a. The richest 1 percent possess over 40 percent of the total national wealth.
    b. The net worth of the richest 1 percent is greater than the bottom 95 percent.
    c. The top 5 percent rules because its money controls the economic, social, political, and cultural spheres and also develops the leaders who control the major corporations and the government.

3. The ruling class controls the majority of information sources;[5] six corporations now control the media.[6] They set the agenda based on corporate values. They support the status quo[7] and distract the public by focusing on entertainment or filtered news.[8]

Ruling-class power is based on the control of political, economic, and social institutions. Below is a glance at some major institutions[9] controlled by the ruling class that help to dominate and exploit the working class.

<u>Corporations</u>. Corporations,[10] hierarchical organizations whose primary purpose is to make money for their stockholders,[11] have become a dominant force in our society.[12] When the US Constitution was approved, we had six corporations. By 2012, we had 8,800.[13] They are composed of the major stockholders and the boards of directors they choose. They decide all matters of production, with no input from employees. They largely manage our food, our clothing, our finances, our transportation, our jobs, our retirement, our health care, our entertainment, our schooling, and our energy needs.[14] The wealth of the 8,800 corporations gives them the power to shape politics to their desire. Corporations play an important role in the political process. After leaving office, government leaders are frequently appointed to corporate boards. Corporations promote think tanks and research institutes to create public policy. They develop and support the most powerful lobbies in both the federal and state governments. They own the mass media, and through advertising, they create and manipulate public consciousness. Since they came to receive the same rights as individuals in 1889[15] and 2010,[16] corporations have substantially increased their power.[17] Corporations have gone beyond our national boundaries and are now

global. A study of over forty-three thousand transnational corporations (TNCs) has identified a relatively small group of companies, mainly banks with disproportionate power over the global economy.[18] Given that corporations need vast sums of money to have representation in Washington, even domestic corporations are at the mercy of the transnational corporations, which have much more money. According to the World Bank in 2011, of the world's top one hundred economies, fifty-three are countries, thirty-four are cities, and thirteen are corporations.[19] One way to see the effect of the power of transnational corporations is to look to their tax status. Corporations paid 50 percent of the federal taxes in World War II and paid less than 10 percent in 2008. Two out of three corporations paid no taxes from 1998 through 2005.[20] One-third of the largest corporations paid zero taxes; some even received credits.[21] In addition, over the past twenty-five years, corporations and wealthy individuals have found new tax havens in which to hide their wealth from taxation.[22] This leaves a larger burden of taxes on the backs of the working class. Even Warren Buffet, one of the richest men in the world, commented that his secretary paid a larger percentage of her income in taxes than he did.[23]

Government. Through personal wealth, corporate wealth, the two-party arrangement, lobbyists, the legal structure, experts, and professionals, the ruling class has power over the government.[24] An example of the convergence of corporations and government is seen in the American Legislative Exchange Council[25] (ALEC), a politically conservative, "nonpartisan" (the members, with the exception of one Democrat, are the elite of the extreme right-wing Republican Party) nonprofit (at taxpayer expense) policy organization. Its membership consists of both state legislators and members of the private sector corporate elite. ALEC advocates for free-market principles, attacks on unions, and limited government and prepares thousands of model bills introduced across the country by legislators.[26] In an Arizona ALEC meeting, among the corporate sponsors were AT&T, State Farm Insurance, Johnson & Johnson, the American Bail Coalition, ExxonMobil, the American Petroleum Institute, and Walmart.[27] Currently, ALEC is losing members due to the bad publicity. There is fluid interaction between members of the government and corporate leaders. The corporate leaders routinely become US ambassadors, and former cabinet members become well-paid consultants. The politicians who control government are generally the ones with the most money.[28] Through the control of government, the ruling class can direct the use of force domestically (the military, the police, and legal system) and internationally (the military). For example, to protect their profits and suppress dissent, the United States maintains 725 military bases around the globe.[29] The United States has, in effect, become a permanent war economy[30] that hurts workers in four ways: (1) it maintains the ruling class hierarchy, placing generals in an isolating, privileged position with no real understanding of the lives of the troops;[31] (2) it supports the most powerful armaments industry in the world (providing fewer jobs than equivalent nonmilitary production); (3) the military eases the movement of corporations to outsource to other countries, leaving the American working class unemployed; and (4) it serves to keep the working class around the world under control.

Political Parties. Having two political parties gives the appearance of competition and the representation of different interests.[32] Noam Chomsky argued that we have one political party with two business wings.[33] Some example are that the candidates in both major political parties support

NAFTA, GATT, the WTO, free trade, the supremacy of Wall Street, the boycott of Cuba, uncritical support of Israel, the militarization and plunder of Africa, the avoidance of climate change treaties, advocacy of "clean coal" and "safe nuclear energy," the war on whistle-blowers, the War on Drugs, the primacy of the national security state, and the unwillingness to enact any sort of WPA-style program to create millions of jobs. Through the use of the Commission on Presidential Debates[34] (a private company), the two parties have prevented third-party candidates representing potential labor or working-class parties from appearing on major public debates. Both of these major parties do not have extensive contact with the working class.[35] Through lobbyists[36] and well-placed friends, the wealthy get access and thus give the legislators a ruling-class view of the issues and problems facing society. Politicians in both parties are wealthy or have access to money, while at the same time, workers do the fighting and dying in wars that maintain the wealth of the ruling class.[37] Andrew Levine best summarizes the party system when he states that the Democrats and Republicans "feed from the same trough, they obey the same masters, and their deeper political inclinations are of a piece."[38]

Legal System. The ruling class creates and modifies the rules by which we live[39] and guarantees that, in any case of conflict, their rules win out in the courts. A class analysis of the Constitution demonstrates that it is a political extension of capitalism.[40] The originators of the Constitution were the influential men of the times—the businessmen, merchants, bankers, land speculators, slave owners, traders, and lawyers. They framed it to give a story of equal rights and responsibilities while ignoring the reality of slavery, women's oppression, and class domination. Recent activist Supreme

Court decisions designed to shape the economy and politics to the advantage of corporations eroded the idealism of the founders. A modern outcome of this bias is demonstrated in the US Supreme Court's 1976 decision in the case *Buckley v. Valeo*, which concluded that money spent to influence elections is a form of constitutionally protected free speech,[41] followed by the Supreme Court ruling in 2010 on the Citizens United case that allowed unlimited corporate funding of independent political advertising. In the end, Citizens United permitted a small group of corporate managers to buy elections in secret, increasing ruling-class control.[42] The judiciary is an important instrument for social, economic, and political control by the ruling class. For the most part, the legal system makes it extremely difficult for ordinary citizens to receive compensation from the harm done to them by corporate actions.[43] The courts have consistently aided business interests by prohibiting strikes, boycotts, and picketing and by issuing injunctions against possible future worker activism and organizing.[44] The courts have been used to sharply curtail the power of unions.[45] Rarely have they actually protected the legal rights of workers.[46] John Jay, the first Supreme Court justice, best stated this relation of the courts to the ruling class when he said, "Those who own the country ought to govern it." The prisons are the final form of social control that the ruling class has over workers. The ruling class uses the threat of prisons to oppress workers and restrict potential disruption to its accumulation process. As jobs are exported or automated, larger numbers of working poor and unemployed rebel and are incarcerated. And while they are in prisons, many inmates are turned into the cheapest form of labor for the capitalist class by corporations like Microsoft, Boeing, and Starbucks.[47] If you're poor, if you're black, or if you're brown, you have a higher chance of ending up in prison.[48] The United States has the largest prison population in the world. Since September 11, 2001, the legal structure pursued a panic mode approaching the scale of the Japanese American internment in World War II. Its actions have led to torture, extraordinary rendition, prolonged detention with no charges or trial, secret imprisonment, and now the right to kill American citizens based on secret evidence. Thousands of US citizens now find themselves on watch lists with no way to challenge them. Government surveillance has grown, leading to ethnic and religious profiling. And the legal system allowed the legislative and executive branches to implement measures like the Patriot Act.[49] The blurring of the line between the police and the military began with the Reagan administration's War on Drugs and has now accelerated with the War on Terror. This change is expressed through the militarization of police, the gutting of the Posse Comitatus Act,[50] excessive growth of SWAT teams, and the purchase of military-grade vehicles, grenade launchers, tanks, heavy-duty weapons, and Predator drones.[51] The public expression of militarization can be seen in images of police dressed in armor and attacking—with chemical weapons—nonviolent, sitting student activists and Wall Street occupiers.[52]

Think Tanks. Think tanks are nonprofit, tax-exempt organizations that combine academics, politics, business, and journalism to produce policy research. They provide experts for testimony on issues in Congress, they publish articles for newspapers, journals, and magazines, their representatives appear on television as policy experts, and they testify on Capitol Hill. They also provide an academic cover to supplement the lobbying of business interests, which promotes research in academia that supports those interests.[53] Since the 1970s, the number of think tanks has tripled.[54] Corporations, foundations, and rich individuals who have close ties to policymakers fund think tanks. There are many more conservative think tanks than liberal ones, since they generally have more money. Some familiar and powerful think tanks are: (centrist) the Brookings Institution, the Council on Foreign Relations, the RAND Corporation; (conservative) American Enterprise Institute, Heritage Foundation, Cato Institute, Center for Strategic and International Studies, Hoover Institution, Heartland Institute; and (progressive) Economic Policy Institute. Though their policies vary depending on their political perspectives, they all generally support capitalism, moderate government regulations, and a foreign policy driven by self-interest.[55]

Media. The media are controlled and run by the capitalist class and spread its worldview.[56] On all the major current events, a unified mass media uncritically supported the US political line: the reaction to the 9/11 attack, the invasion of Iraq, Iran's nuclear program, Israel's aggression, and the bailout of Wall Street. The media are traditionally anti-working class.[57] When the working class reacts to oppression, the media point out the danger of a class war rather than a chance for workers to change their conditions.[58] When the media expose corruption, it is touted as proof that the system works (but rarely that the system is at fault). Even the internet, once hoped to be a free source of information for citizens, is facing a lack of government regulation, leading to a connection between economic power and the digital world, which naturally results in domination by the views and values of large corporations.[59]

Schools. Class-analysis approach sees schooling as one method of maintaining order by socializing students into accepting many values and attitudes of the ruling class.

With our country's move from an agricultural to an industrial economy, potential workers were pulled away from family ties, sent to schools, and taught punctuality, competitiveness, and respect for authority (remember the bells in elementary school?). Schools were almost entirely in the hands of the capitalist class.[60] The working class and labor unions supported public school, because education was seen as a way out and up.[61] We currently have a new generation of working-class students dropping out or graduating with inferior skills. This reflects the changing needs of the ruling class. Automation, outsourcing, privatization, simpler service jobs, and the move from a postindustrial, high-technology, information economy to financial, real estate, and speculative capital doesn't require a large, educated, housed, and healthy labor force, so state policy reduced spending on education, health services, and housing. Covering up this policy shift has been the conservative mantra that "throwing money at the schools" (or whatever public institution that is in crisis) will not solve the problem. In contrast to decaying public schools for the working class, the ruling class has its own educational structure designed to maintain its power and control: private schools,[62] elite universities, universities doing military research, the correct fraternities and sororities, and an extensive group of clubs and activities that are found in the Social Register.[63]

Of course, the ruling class is not a monolith. There are differing sectors within it. According to Jeffrey Sachs,[64] there are four major sectors: (1) the military-industrial complex, (2) the Wall Street–Washington complex, (3) the Big Oil transport–military complex, and (4) the health care industry. In addition, there are the prison-industrial complex, the mercantile interests, and the manufacturing interests. Although these sectors are often not in general agreement about economic issues, they cover up internal struggles and weaknesses by exhibiting a public class solidarity through media pronouncements, business connections, interlocking directorships, belonging to the same social clubs (the Bohemian Grove and Skull and Bones),[65] living in the same gated communities, eating at the same restaurants, vacationing in the same resorts, intermarrying, and going to the same private schools.

Ruling-class solidarity is currently being tested due to the worldwide economic crisis, the transition from productive to financial capitalism, and the ensuing panic of our leading financial institutions. This growth of institutional collapse and inequality is producing elite that, due to their social distance from the working class, hold on to a culture of corruption that condition them to be incompetent and unable to reproduce the system that produces a ruling class.[66] In addition, we have the loss of easy access to cheap energy that previously buoyed our economic success and maintained the power of the ruling class (see chapter 9). These conditions have led the ruling class (1) to accelerate and intensify the class war by attacking labor and any advantages and protection that the working class has gained;[67] (2) to undermine its earlier solidarity in a rush for short-term profits, becoming more interested in exploiting capitalism rather than preserving it (when it seems that the ship is in danger of sinking, the rats scurry to save themselves); and (3) to find new ways to hide its wealth.[68]

What about Small Business?

The problem with the rat race is that even if you win, you're still a rat.

—Lily Tomlin

How does the two-class structure explain the role of small-business owners who work for themselves or who hire a few employees[69]—the small–grocery store owner, the auto-shop mechanic, the massage therapist, the hardware-store owner, the beautician, and so on? If they have employees and work for themselves, they play a double role. On the one hand, insofar as they work for a living, they are in the working class, and insofar as they manage and live off of the work of their employees, they are capitalists, although not socially powerful ones (except over the lives of their employees). The majority of small-business owners maintain the same values that the capitalist class does, since they are in competition with other capitalists for profits and survival. They treat their employees similarly by giving them back a portion of the value of what they produced. However, because so many small businesses are not as profitable or secure as the large corporations they compete with, their employees usually do not have the benefits the unions fought for in the struggles with the large corporations.

Fortunately, there are some small businesses, co-ops, and nonprofits—due to personal ties to their communities, their customers, and their employees—which modify the profit-dominated values of business by including a concern for the needs of both employees and community; however, they are the exception.[70]

Being your own boss and starting your own business is a dream of countless Americans. It goes along with the belief that if you work hard enough, you will succeed, and if you do not succeed, it is your fault. This perspective supports the individualistic orientation of our culture as well as diverting the blame for the failure of small business on individual entrepreneurs rather than looking to the structure of capitalism.

Why is it that, according to the US Small Business Administration, 80 percent of all small businesses fail within the first five years? Most surveys blame the failure rate on lack of skills, lack of sales, poor financial control, lack of start-up capital, and so on. It seems that the high failure rate of small business is due to lack of business and management knowledge. Much of this is probably true, but a class analysis would ask questions about the relationship between small business and the competition of large corporations, such as Walmart, Barnes & Noble, Home Depot, General Motors, ExxonMobil, Ford,

General Electric, and so on. These giants, which employ millions, are responsible for small businesses often being driven to bankruptcy through monopolistic pricing and predatory practices. Small-business owners have no control over the costs and expenses of loans, of their equipment, or of the rent they pay. These are controlled by the big businesses that set policies and lobby governments at all levels to their advantage. What happened to the independent bookstores when Barnes & Noble, Amazon, and Borders entered the market? (And by 2011, even Borders disappeared). What happened to small retail stores in communities around our country when Walmart entered the picture?[71]

The hope of success in the transition from worker to small-business owner leads one to hold on to the dream that we can all individually make it in America if we try, that individualism rather than collective action can allow for success, and that the ladder to the top is available to all. But the fact remains that a small-business owner who wants to start a business runs into an almost insurmountable problem—competition against much larger corporations who are able to manipulate the system through an army of lobbyists who are able to create loopholes and contrive ways of paying fewer taxes. It would seem ridiculous to most of us if a friend decided to compete against AT&T with a new telephone company or against Toyota with a new automobile company, but less-extreme variations of this approach are being tried every day with the results in bankruptcies for the majority of those attempts.[72]

The dream of opening a small business is a different way of stating that being in the working class is unfulfilling, alienating, and hopeless.

CHAPTER 6

The Excluded and Abused Workers

Farm workers do the hardest work in this country, yet they're always belittled. The farmworker is forgotten, unknown.

—Frank LeGrande, a ninety-one-year-old farm-labor contractor born in Haiti

Lettuce-cutting and packing was a craft that demanded incredible skill ... In the late 1970s, lechugeros *[lettuce workers] made $12 an hour ... in today's wages, making them among the highest-paid members of the US working class.*

—Frank Bardacke, worker and author

My father arrived from Crete in 1914 and worked in coal mines in West Virginia, Pennsylvania, and Wyoming. He was among the 450,000 Greek immigrants arriving in the United States between 1890 and 1917. In Crete, he was a member of a large peasant family barely surviving on subsistence agriculture in a remote village in the mountains. When crops failed or the economy declined, he, like many Greeks and other Europeans, moved to the New World for economic opportunity. In their transition to America, a few immigrants worked as farm laborers, but most moved to the

Northeast's urban centers and took on work at the bottom of the labor food chain: as unskilled laborers, factory laborers, peddlers, food service workers, small-business owners, railroad and mine workers, and some as indentured servants.[1] This was their path to acceptance into America.

The 1960 CBS documentary *Harvest of Shame* exposed the inhumane conditions under which agricultural migrants labored. These conditions, while shocking to me, were understood and experienced by my father and his friends. But after suffering the initial rejection by the larger society, most European immigrants were eventually tolerated and allowed to become part of the worker movement.

But who took their place? Who did the work at the bottom end of the labor food chain? Who could not organize without facing retaliation? Who could not bargain collectively to transform their workplace conditions or access basic labor protections? Who was not welcomed into the labor movement by the existing worker's organizations and unions that were populated by those previously rejected European immigrants? These were the excluded workers[2] who suffered a more virulent form of racism and structural rejection than was faced by the European immigrants. These are the former African slaves and immigrants from Latin America, Asia, Africa, the Near East, and the Caribbean. They work as farm workers (1.5 million), domestic workers (2 million), and hundreds of thousand food-service workers, guest workers, day laborers, taxi drivers, and workfare workers. The nature and precariousness of their work doesn't allow easy statistics, but theorists suggest that they are growing at a faster rate than other sectors of the job market.

Excluded workers are victims of the legacy of racial prohibitions in US labor law that exempted farm and domestic workers from protection by the National Labor Relations Act[3] as well as the various laws and national origins quotas that Asian, African, and eastern and southern European immigrants faced. These excluded workers do not fit neatly in the traditional depictions of workers. They are excluded from today's labor laws and union-organizing campaigns.[4] They are restaurant employees who are called "tipped workers," excluded from minimum wage laws; taxi drivers, called "independent contractors," excluded from labor protections of being employees; prison inmates[5] given a pittance for their labor by companies on contract with the growing prison complex.[6] They are workfare workers, defined as welfare recipients. They are domestic workers,[7] including nannies[8] and farm workers, who are constantly threatened, forced to work long hours, and cheated out of their wages, housed and transported in remote or inaccessible and dangerous conditions, and in some cases bound by servitude to the employer to whom they are indebted.[9]

Since excluded workers are on the bottom; they are easily ignored and controlled. Their precarious status makes it dangerous for them to even claim their guaranteed rights and benefits. They are the new models of how to treat all workers.

What Is the Underclass?

If you belong to the underclass, you are already guilty.

—Mason Cooley

In *Nickel and Dimed*,[10] Barbara Ehrenreich presented the heartbreaking stories of the working poor: waitresses, Walmart salespersons, house cleaners, nursing home aides, hotel maids, and dishwashers—the greatest victims of the inequities in class society. However, another victimized group is excluded from class society: the underclass, previously known as the *lumpenproletariat*. This group consists of the outcasts that make up a section of the population of industrial centers. It includes the long-term unemployed who will never be rehired, beggars, prostitutes, gangsters, racketeers, petty criminals, tramps, the homeless, the mentally and physically disabled, undocumented aliens, and persons who have been cast out by society, by their families, or by industry. In times of prolonged crisis (depression), innumerable young people who cannot find an opportunity to enter into the society as producers are also pushed into this limbo of the outcast.

The lack of jobs available for workers has created an underground economy where the marginalized population barely survives.[11] The underclass survives in a different way than the working class, mostly by scrounging through the discards of the society. A few survive through the methods and ethical conduct similar to that of the ruling capitalist class. They just don't have the veneer of respectability or control of the important institutions (police, army, business, media, education) to rationalize their acts. Some in the underclass, in trying to survive, are fixated on accumulating wealth by preying on the working class, the group physically closest to them. Most in the underclass are the discards that don't fit in to the value structure of capitalism. They also serve as a warning to the coordinators, traditional working class, and excluded workers to stay in line, accept what your bosses give or tell you, and follow the rules, or else you may end up homeless, dumpster diving, or begging in the streets!

After the economic crisis of 2008, corporations recovered, but for the working class, it was a "jobless recovery."[12] Capitalists found new ways to make money by crushing unions, thinning out their job forces through technology, smart machines, automation, outsourcing, temp work, hiring workers as outside contractors, making the remaining workers work harder and faster, and ignoring workers altogether by making money without producing commodities through the use of financial manipulations (see appendix 2).

Unless those on the bottom organize and rise up, the underclass will be the fastest-growing group of discontented former workers ripe for rebellion, much like the working class of Germany that led to Nazism. The current power of capital and weakness of labor makes it politically unlikely that the underclass will get the relief they got when FDR intervened in the Great Depression and opened up the public sector to workers with the New Deal. Among the early varied reactions to our current state of affairs is the rekindling of labor push back through strikes,[13] the creation of the corporate-created Tea Party,[14] and the Occupy movement that was inspired by the Arab Spring.[15]

What about Gender and Race?[16]

If sex and race are pulled away from class, virtually all that remains is the truncated, provincial, sectarian politics of the white male metropolitan Left.
—Selma James

I am an invisible man. I am a man of substance, of flesh and bone, fiber and liquids—and I might even be said to possess a mind. I am invisible, understand, simply because people refuse to see me.
—Ralph Ellison

We as a nation must undergo a radical revolution of values... when machines and computers, profit motives and property rights, are considered more important than people, the giant triplets of racism, materialism, and militarism are incapable of being conquered.
—Martin Luther King Jr.

Since the 1960s, there has been an increase in the concern about social oppression related more to identity than class (race, gender, disability, sexual orientation, AIDS, homelessness, etc.). At the same time, the labor movement was weakening, further reducing awareness of the importance of class in our society.

This state of affairs has led some in the struggle for equity, justice, and acceptance to argue that the spotlight on class was too focused on the economic structure (the job, the factory, the corporation or industry) to address their search for real satisfaction and recognition in society. They pointed out that women and people of color were less advantaged than white men, regardless of class, in their access to material goods, power, status, and potential for self-actualization and that the working class had ignored the role of the nurturing and reproduction—the unpaid work of women.

In response, advocates of class analysis argue that groups that fight to overcome racism, sexism, and other forms of oppression too often assume their struggle can be achieved within the confines of capitalism, as they see little connection between the structure of capitalism and their concerns. Class analysis argues that oppression can be better understood when it is connected to exploitation and dehumanization of workers through the wage system. But class analysis also acknowledges that racism, sexism, and all forms of oppression have damaged everyone, and their effects reside in our culture and individual character structures. We need to unlearn[17] those oppressions as we unify in our struggle to create a classless society. The advocates of class analysis argue that they do address sexism and racism—but as structural problems.

Another criticism of the working-class perspective is that it incorrectly assumes that class is prior to or more important than race, gender, and so on. Evidence for this argument is that a lot of unions excluded women and people of color from joining their ranks in the early union movement,[18] and currently, they argue that class analysis doesn't adequately focus on the brutal economic realities of globalization where women bear a greater burden of labor throughout the world as social services have been cut. Women are subject to sexual violence and in much of the world are not allowed to control their own processes of reproduction.

People of color are currently unemployed in greater numbers than whites, are paid less, oppressed more, and held in jails in higher proportion than the population. And finally, there is little or no recognition of white privilege[19] and to what W. E. B. Du Bois identified as the "psychological wage of whiteness" where whites (especially poor whites) hang on to the psychological advantage of believing their "whiteness" makes them superior to people of color, even though they are suffering economically.[20]

Class analysis doesn't focus adequately on the prevailing sexism and racism in our country and the world, since it fails to demonstrate how class itself was infected by patriarchy and racism.

Some Historical Examples

1. Silvia Federici pointed out that the burning of the "witches"[21] in the late Middle Ages was a systematic attempt by the then ruling class to deprive women of the power they held prior to the enclosure movement and turn them into labor reproducers and subordinate to men as well as a source of cheap or free labor.
2. In addition, we can see that the creation of class required the prior subordination of Africans. Theodore William Allen argued that the "white race" was invented by the ruling class in response to labor unrest manifested in Bacon's Rebellion[22] of 1676–77, where racial privileges for white workers were deliberately instituted as a response to the potential solidarity of black and white workers.
3. Workingmen in the North, in their attempt to maintain their social position, made sure to differentiate themselves from the slaves of the South. They asserted that the labor they did for wages was the opposite of slavery, which promoted the illusion that wage labor was free labor and appeared as a progressive development. But actually, the difference between slave labor and wage labor is that in slavery, the worker is sold, and in wage labor, the worker is rented.
4. Eric Williams also demonstrated that slavery financed the Industrial Revolution and was the social frame that created the waged working class itself.[23] According to new evidence

by Robin Blackburn,[24] the slave trade provided between 20.9 and 55 percent of Britain's gross fixed capital formation.
5. Douglas A. Blackmon[25] pointed out the persistence of slavery under the name of debt peonage (being thrown in jail for an alleged debt and forced to be a laborer without pay) from the emancipation until the civil rights movement of the 1960s (some argue that it is still going on in some hidden areas in the South). In this time, millions of African Americans lived in fear that they and their families would become debt victims. The former slaveholders created the condition of peonage in order to exploit the labor of the former slaves. The psychological and social damage caused was devastating and still influences the culture of black people.[26] Blackmon concludes his book with the following:

> Only by acknowledging the full extent of slavery's grip on U.S. society—its intimate connections to present-day wealth and power, the depth of its injury to millions of black Americans, the shocking nearness in time of its true end—can we reconcile the paradoxes of current American life.

Class analysis's structural approach is a necessary but not sufficient condition for the elimination of oppression. Race and gender oppression has an important effect on class, but it existed historically prior to or concurrent with the development of the industrial working class. Class analysis must support, learn from, and address identity groups' strategies for overcoming sexism, racism, and all other types of oppression, while linking those struggles to the class structure of capitalism.

| Seeing Through The System |

What about the Disrespect of Common People?

Let me tell you about the very rich. They are different from you and me. They possess and enjoy early, and it does something to them, makes them soft where we are hard, and cynical where we are trustful, in a way that, unless you were born rich, it is very difficult to understand. They think, deep in their hearts, that they are better than we are because we had to discover the compensations and refuges of life for ourselves. Even when they enter deep into our world or sink below us, they still think that they are better than we are. They are different.

—F. Scott Fitzgerald

Band and tribal society focused on living in relative harmony with nature and gave rise to a way of thinking that reflected the similarity of everyone's experiences. Class society manipulated nature, was complex and hierarchical, and gave rise to a division of labor with a matching shift in thinking. Class society required intensive manual labor to carry out the planting, herding, maintenance, harvesting, and storing of food. The slaves and common people performed this work. It also required another smaller group to manage, coordinate, and plan those tasks. The shift in thinking in class society reflected the separation of labor: manual and mental.

Slaves and common people did the manual work, while the overseers, who focused on planning and organizing, did the mental work. In ancient Athens, the hierarchy of mind over matter was depicted in the writings of the philosophers. For example, Plato's Allegory of the Cave asserted that thoughts, based on the perfect unchanging forms (mental entities) that were not part of the physical world, were more valuable and true than the impermanence and illusion of daily life—the changing physical world. This preference of mental over material reality was modified by the Christians of the Middle Ages, where God/perfection—the equivalent of Plato's forms—was contrasted to the sinful body that decayed and died—the equivalent of material reality. Today, our society expresses that dichotomy in valuing mental over manual labor as expressed in the higher status of thinkers and managers over laborers.

Before Plato, one of the earliest literary depictions of common people as mindless bodies was by Homer in *The Iliad*,[27] when he described the commoner Thersites as a bowlegged, lame, ugly hunchback. Homer portrayed him as a vulgar man whose "head was full of obscenities, teeming with rant." Thersites had risen and spoken against King Agamemnon, exposing the Trojan War for what it was—a foolish search for glory, power, women, and gold by the ruling princes while the common soldiers died. Both Odysseus and Achilles (who were ruling-class warriors) beat him to put him in his place. Thersites's place was to take orders and fight, not to think or complain. Because of the importance and influence of *The Iliad* in Western civilization, we can see a continuation of Thersites's treatment in the history of our society.

A modern example of the mental/manual separation can be demonstrated in the practice of Fredrick Taylor (1856–1915), who developed a structure named after him, "Taylorism,"—also called the scientific management of work—in the beginning of the twentieth century. In order to increase production and job efficiency in factories, Taylor developed a method of divorcing the worker from the skills and knowledge of the work process—separating the worker's mind from his or her body. After studying the particular work process in factories and breaking it down into its parts, management would use "scientific techniques" to exclude all "unnecessary" movements, determining the most efficient way to complete the process. Later, management, representing mental labor, would tell the workforce, who represent manual labor, how to do their tasks. In this way, Taylorism turned workers into objects like any other part of the production process; they became parts of a machine, easily replaceable. Charlie Chaplin's film *Modern Times* was a penetrating critique of Taylorism.[28]

This depiction of workers as stupid but strong is reflected on television. For example, *All in the Family, Married ... with Children, The Simpsons,* or programs like *The Jerry Springer Show,* all depict the working class as being intellectually inferior or solely involved with bodily functions, similar to Homer's depiction of Thersites.[29]

In addition to intellectually disempowering the working class and morally demeaning them, the ruling capitalist class uses media and its domination of government to maintain control through the use of panic[30] as a tool of propaganda. By maintaining a high level of fear through shocking presentations of crime waves, drug violence, health epidemics, child abductions, warfare (Grenada, Libya, Nicaragua, Desert Storm, the "axis of evil," Afghanistan, the War on Terror), the working class is overwhelmed and thus more easily controlled. Often, the excessive concern for security and safety, as articulated in the speeches of our politicians, rapidly assembled laws, and pronouncements by the government, indicate a need to control or cower the population. The working class can be fooled for a while, as many were in the invasion of Vietnam[31] and Iraq, but as in the case of Thersites—who could see what was going on in the Trojan War—workers who experience oppressive power and disrespect know that something is wrong.

When the ruling capitalist class, through the control of ideas and information, is able to scare and convince the working class that they are stupid,[32] it has another rationale for directing the production process. This control is often accomplished with the blessing of the employees themselves, since many have internalized the widespread depictions of themselves as lesser, not important enough or smart enough to deserve to be a force in society. How often I have heard workers say, "Hell, I just work to keep bread on the table. I don't care about any of that crap they talk about in the paper, except for the sports page."

The lives of the majority of working people require a rigorous, sophisticated coordination of physical and mental work under difficult conditions. Barbara Ehrenreich[33] found, in contrast to the social myth that workers are stupid and lazy, that they are filled with intelligence, tenacity, and generosity, in spite of being exploited. They are able to successfully perform the lowliest occupations, requiring exhausting mental and muscular efforts. After her experience as a worker, acquired as part of the research for her book, Ehrenreich found that no job is "unskilled."[34]

At first glance, the historical disrespect of workers by the ruling class–controlled media seems to have been reversed by the mass media's reaction toward working people after the 9/11 terrorist strikes in New York City. It took that tragedy to get the media to recognize and celebrate the power, solidarity, and compassion of the working class. New York police and firefighters were cheered at sports events and applauded on TV shows.

The celebration of the working class was temporary and was focused on the firefighters and police, who became celebrities, heroic warriors saving us from total destruction by going into the burning towers. The rest—the construction, medical, restaurant, and sanitation workers—got much less recognition. The undocumented laborers, who worked at the least desirable and hardest jobs of cleaning up, were ignored. It seems as if giving up your life in a spectacular heroic act is the only way workers are noticed and valued.

During the anthrax scare in 2001, the government focused on the politicians and their staffs and ignored the postal employees, who were primarily black.[35] This was an example of the old idea that workers are not important and that people of color are less human.[36]

Reports of toxic poisoning of workers who cleaned up the Twin Towers site have been ignored by the authorities and by the public.[37] This lack of concern forced some of the workforce at the Twin Towers' site to organize in order to protect themselves[38] as workers have done throughout the history of industrial capitalism. In fact, worker revolts have been an important way to gain rights and advance their lives—for example, the fight for the eight-hour workday, the weekend, health care, safe work environments, retirement, and vacations.

The historic disrespect and outright absence of the lives of the working class in literature is expressed in the following excerpt from a poem titled "Questions from a Worker Who Reads" by Bertolt Brecht.

> *Who built Thebes of the seven gates?*
> *In the books you will find the names of kings.*
> *Did the kings haul up the lumps of rock?*
>
> *The young Alexander conquered India.*
> *Was he alone?*

The disrespect of the common worker is reflected in the way they are absent from most histories. The master narrative taught in public schools sees the United States as the freest, most open, opportunity-filled nation on earth, while it fails to talk about the tightening of the bonds of slavery, the denial of the citizenship for women, the confinement of wage earners, and the seizing of Native American lands and killing its inhabitants. As Edward Countryman has observed, "The glory did not come free. It had a price, and Americans ought to be comfortable enough with ourselves to recognize that the price and the glory cannot be pried apart."[39]

Michael Parenti described three types of history in *History as Mystery*: mainstream history, dissident history, and real history.[40] Mainstream history is the dominant version of reality reflecting the interests of the elite. It is the history presented by "textbook authors, mainstream academicians, political leaders, government officials, and news and entertainment media."[41] This is sometimes called the great man theory and focuses on rulers or leaders and credits all advances to them.

Dissident history is the history from below. It is composed of the stories of those who are ignored by mainstream history—the working class, women, people of color, and so forth. The excerpt in the above poem by Brecht may be seen as a call for a dissident history of the world that includes the working class.

Real history challenges some assumptions of mainstream history by reframing them. Parenti stated, "Rather than debating whether it was Christopher Columbus, Lief Ericson, or Amerigo Vespucci who discovered America, real history argues that the Western Hemisphere was not 'discovered' but invaded in a series of brutal conquests that brought destruction to millions of indigenous inhabitants and hundreds of cultures."[42] Real history takes in the insights of mainstream history and of dissident history and adds the interconnection of events. Real history, for example, recognizes that you cannot understand the rise of Christianity without considering the rise and fall of the Roman Empire, or you cannot understand the workers' movements in the nineteenth century without considering the Industrial Revolution.

Class analysis supports real history in that it reframes the descriptions of society presented by mainstream history and dissident history through the lens of class conflict. This is done by paying attention to the struggle between common people, trying to survive and thrive in changing conditions, and the rulers who try to maintain their control and power over them. Howard Zinn's *A People's History of the United States: 1492 to Present* is an excellent example of real history. Unlike mainstream historians, who look at history through the lives of presidents and generals, Zinn looks at history from the point of view of those on the margins: women, blacks, Indians, poor laborers, fugitive slaves, war resisters, and so on. In this way, he illustrates how ordinary people make change. An important addition to Zinn's social history is an economic history from a class perspective. In *Accumulation and Power: An Economic History of the United States*, Richard Du Boff argues that to understand our economy, we need to understand how it evolved. His book helps provide this understanding.[43]

Class and Culture in Cold War America: A Rainbow at Midnight[44] by George Lipsitz is another excellent example of real history, history from the standpoint of class analysis. In this book, he demonstrates how the capitalist class, in striving to contain a massive increase in strikes after World War II, promoted the passage of four programs: (1) the Taft-Hartley Act (1947), that was supported under the pretense of promoting labor relations but was actually designed to minimize the power of the workforce by strengthening union leaders and tying them to the goals of capitalism; (2) the Marshall Plan (1947), which gave the appearance of being the European recovery act but was an attempt by the capitalist class to restore world markets and maintain their profits and defend the devastated nations from the competing economic system of the Soviet Union; (3) the red scare, which aimed to eliminate the proworker forces that seemed to be modeled after the peoples' revolution in the feared USSR; and (4) the continuation of the militarized war economy into the postwar era, achieved through the so-called Cold War that claimed to give jobs to the underemployed to maintain national security but was designed to diminish the growing clout of the working class by reducing the power of unions.

All of these programs, in spite of their public pronouncements, were partly designed to curb the potential power and threat of the working class to the ruling capitalist class. None of the mainstream histories that I was exposed to in my schooling ever looked at the postwar era from Lipsitz's perspective. Mainstream history texts ignore class and the economy. In an important study of history textbooks,[45] it was found that discussions of economic and political inequality were ignored. While exaggerating the glories of free enterprise, these texts rarely used the terms "capitalism" or "class conflicts," and they never explained how the American economy operated.

Imagine how our minds are controlled by the history we learn. In my schooling, I was led to believe the following: (1) unions were composed of selfish bullies, violent strikers, and self-serving leaders and needed to be controlled; (2) the Marshall Plan was a great gift to Europe due to American generosity; (3) we needed military buildups because of the threat of the Soviet Union at the end of World War II; and (4) the military-industrial complex (made famous by Eisenhower in his farewell speech) provided the American workforce with the greatest postwar boom that created the "middle class" and made our country the envy of the world.[46] Although I believe three and four contained some truth, they did not tell the whole story.

By rights, we in the United States should actually celebrate the then Soviet Union (now Russia) since it used our equipment while sacrificing millions of its people to defeat fascism that saved millions of American lives. In addition, the Soviet Union's existence as a "worker's state"[47] forced our society to give our workers a better deal in order to demonstrate the superiority of our system (witness the decline of the US labor movement since we "won" the Cold War and the Soviet Union was no longer our competitor).

Most history is mainstream history, and we are taught to think, see, feel, and act from the perspective of its advocates.[48] In every period in the history of class society, the slaves, serfs, peasants, workers, and the business class have fought with their rulers, but since the rulers won, they got to write that history.

Imagine how our understanding of ourselves and of our world would be changed by substituting terms as slave society for ancient society (Greece and Rome) and serf society for medieval society and wage-labor society for modern industrial society. Our historians would be forced to reframe the stories of aristocrats and leaders by including how the economy worked, which in turn would force a new understanding of the politics of those societies, as well as depict the daily struggle of the common people.

Here are some prominent examples in history where common people challenged authority for the right to rule themselves that we can now reframe:
- the slave revolts in Greece and Rome—Spartacus is the well-known example

- Toussaint-Louverture and the Haitian Revolution in 1794
- in the United States—Shays' Rebellion in 1786, Gabriel Prosser in 1800, Denmark Vesey in 1822, Nat Turner in 1831, and *La Amistad* in 1839
- the peasant uprisings in France (1358), England (1381), Hungary (1514), Germany (1524), and Russia (1670)
- the free urban workers in Florence (1378), Paris (1588)
- the emerging business class in the American Revolution (1776), and French Revolution (1789)
- the peasants with the help of a small, disciplined working class—in the Chinese Revolution (1911 and 1949), the Russian Revolution (1917), and the Cuban Revolution (1959)

But even this reframing is not sufficient for a class analysis, because many of the rebellions and revolutions that were described as worker or peasant revolts were carried out in the name of nationalism and patriotism, that, as Emma Goldman stated,

> assumes that our globe is divided into little spots, each surrounded by an iron gate. Those who had the fortune of being born on some particular spot, consider themselves better, nobler, grander, and more intelligent than the living beings inhabiting any other spot.

But even this imperfect reframing at least points to the common working people as significant actors in world history and can lead to their recognition and respect. In the United States, one way workers fought for recognition and respect was the union movement, discussed next.

CHAPTER 7
Unions

Unions are the deformed offspring of capitalism.
—Daniel Johnson

With all their faults, trade unions have done more for humanity than any other organization of men that ever existed. They have done more for decency, for honesty, for education, for the betterment of the race, for the developing of character in men, than any other association of men.
—Clarence Darrow

Throughout much of its history, the AFL-CIO and other U.S. labor organizations have worked with CIA and multi-national corporations to overthrow democratically-elected governments, collaborated with dictators against progressive labor movements, supported reactionary labor movements against progressive governments, worked with corporate America to organize racist and protectionist campaigns against foreign countries, and encouraged racist campaigns against immigrant workers.
—Lee Siu Hin

After the revolution, the new United States was transformed from an agricultural to an industrial society, where the sons of farmers, discharged soldiers, and immigrants came to the growing industrialized cities of the North. These new arrivals only had their labor to offer, while the capitalists owned the tools, buildings, and raw materials. Using this advantage, capitalists tried to maximize their profits by pushing the working class to work longer hours, cutting their wages, and exploiting child and female labor.

The American working class was weak, compared to the working class in Europe because of these reasons: (1) it was weakened by divisions between whites and African Americans and later by the division between skilled (generally northern European Protestants) and industrial laborers (generally eastern and southern European Catholics and Jews); (2) workers were unable to develop their own political party, since the electoral structure and rules imposed by the two major parties made it difficult for the formation of third parties; (3) they had difficulty organizing due to the employer-influenced government practices, police arrests, and court injunctions; (4) they were bucking the American tradition of free-market liberalism, which attacked any actions that could be characterized as restraint of trade or interference of private property; and (5) they lived in a political system that seemed to promote their political freedoms, yet they were handcuffed in the workplace where they labored under the unquestioned power of the bosses to supply a market.[1]

But unlike the extreme conditions in Europe, with an overabundance of labor and a scarcity of land, in the New World, there was a relative scarcity of labor and the possibility for peasants to find land for farming, so the working class was able to push back. In fact, the wages of the working class rose through most of the nineteenth and twentieth centuries (see appendix 2). But the push back came with consequences, making the class conflict in America more ruthless and violent than it was in Europe, because the business class was more powerful in America than in Europe.

Since the capitalist class had more power than the working class, it was able to impose inadequate wages, long hours, and unsafe working conditions, forcing the workforce to find ways to organize and fight for their rights. Workers' reactions began sporadically in the eighteenth century. The growth of the populist movement, industrialism, and reactions to the inequality of the Gilded Age (the late nineteenth century) led to the beginning of the union movement. If there is one thing to remember from this story, it is that unions were created as a defensive action to counter the oppressive power and excess wealth accumulation of the capitalist/owning class. This class war has gone on for the whole of capitalism's existence, sometimes hidden by the propaganda of the capitalist class but persistently there.

The capitalists reacted to the union movement in a variety of ways: outright denunciation by declaring a class war; qualified acceptance as a way to manage their labor force by corrupting or buying off the union leadership; using the capitalists' control of education and media to feed the public the message that militant unions are full of corruption, violence, and greed; and putting "uncooperative" unions on the defensive. A few capitalists recognized that unionization leads to higher productivity, lower turnover, better workplace communication, and better-trained employees.[2]

The union movement has been responsible for more pay and better benefits for unionized as well as nonunionized employees. Unions have given workers a sense of community, power, and dignity. Unions are primarily responsible for the eight-hour day, the forty-hour week, time and a half for overtime, better conditions in the workplace, health care, unemployment insurance, vacations, child labor laws, environmental laws, and retirement benefits. These "benefits" were fought for and not generously given by the capitalists.[3] And currently, as the union movement has been weakened, as union jobs have been lost through automation and outsourcing, the benefits are being taken away.

In the United States, the attempts by unions to organize the labor force fell between the extremes of two paths. The American

Federation of Labor (formed in 1886) represented the first and most accommodating path. For them, the purpose of a union was to provide organized, reliable, and obedient employees who would accept slogans like "a fair day's wage for a fair day's work." In addition, they viewed unions as organizations that could gain

1. a counterbalance to the unchecked power of employers;
2. respect on the job;
3. better wages and benefits;
4. more flexibility for work and family needs; and
5. a voice in improving the quality of their products and services.[4]

This perspective led to an improvement in the lives of many working people. But since it accepted the logic of the system (the necessity of exploitation) and hierarchy, it saw the worker's labor power as a product (commodity) to be bought in the labor market as any other commodity. Instead of organizing to transform society into a socially just arrangement, these unions were an extension of corporate capitalism. They accepted the status quo and used it to gain as much as they could for their members.[5]

The second path can be seen in the preamble to the constitution of the International Workers of the World (IWW), formed in 1905, some of which is reproduced below.

> The working class and the employing class have nothing in common. There can be no peace so long as hunger and want are found among millions of the working people, and the few, who make up the employing class, have all the good things of life.
>
> Between these two classes a struggle must go on until the workers of the world organize as a class, take possession of the means of production, abolish the wage system, and live in harmony with the Earth.

> Instead of the conservative motto, "A fair day's wage for a fair day's work," we must inscribe on our banner the revolutionary watchword, "Abolition of the wage system."
>
> It is the historic mission of the working class to do away with capitalism. The army of production must be organized, not only for everyday struggle with capitalists, but also to carry on production when capitalism shall have been overthrown. By organizing industrially we are forming the structure of the new society within the shell of the old.[6]

This preamble has a refreshing clarity and focus: its overt attack on the wages, its unrelenting fight for the emancipation of the working class from capitalism, its advocacy for transferring the ownership and control of the means of production and distribution to unions. These are radical positions not acceptable to the status quo, and their fulfillment requires a revolution. So naturally, there was push back by government, industry, and even other unions. That, along with its own factional disputes and antiracist and profemale policies (that were not acceptable to the majority of citizens in the early years of the twentieth century) and a few successful major strikes, its opposition to the US participation in World War I—as well as its advocacy of strikes in war-related industries—resulted in its persecution by the federal government during World War I. By 1920, continuing government repression led to the downfall of the IWW as an effective force for labor (although it still exists today and is growing).[7]

Although many labor unions give the workforce a unified voice that allows them to fight for a share of the economic growth they help create, they are still losing the class war because of the following:

1. They have accepted their subordinate role in the economic

structure, which requires they be exploited by the capitalist class.
2. Union membership continuously drops.
3. The United States has one of the highest levels of income inequality, one of the major indicators of union weakness,[8] and is one of a few developed countries where inequality has increased so radically since 1980.[9]
4. The rich and corporations, using their political power, have radically lowered their income tax burden since 1945, both absolutely and relative to the tax burdens of the working class;[10] currently nearly two-thirds of major corporations pay no taxes at all. Among them are ExxonMobil, Bank of America, General Electric, Chevron, Boeing, Valero Energy, Goldman Sachs, Citigroup, and ConocoPhillips.[11]
5. The power of the strike, historically one of the key weapons unions used to get good wages and working conditions from employers, has practically disappeared due to the accumulation of antiunion laws and practices developed by industry and government.[12] The major US strikes, involving one thousand workers or more, fell to just five in 2009, the lowest level since 1947.[13] Currently, due to the increasingly dire conditions for the workforce, there is some worker fight back against the increasing oppression and exploitation by the capitalist class.[14]
6. There has been an organized attack on unions that was instigated by the powerful antiunion movement in the business community and assisted by weak legal protections of labor.[15]
7. Running a business is easier than running a trade union. Businesses have one purpose: to maximize profit. But unions are voluntary organizations composed of many individuals with many interests and perspectives. Their members have different skills and needs. There is a continuing tension within unions between the interests of the shop floor

and those of the union bureaucracy. Compared to the undemocratic command and control structure of business, unions are easily broken.

These are some additional explanations as to why unions are getting weaker.

1. Since the 1970s, the capitalists have been getting stronger (see appendix 2) and are able to systematically shift wealth from the working class to the capitalist class and, with that power, impose their will on to government and labor.
2. The deindustrialization and the shipping of jobs to union-unfriendly areas like the South or other countries has become more prevalent due to increased competition with other economies and the search for new markets.
3. Usage of machines and robot technology to replace employees has increased.
4. Because of the current economic crisis, lack of jobs, and the growing anti-immigrant hysteria, unions are perceived as less relevant.
5. Some unions don't pay enough attention to the more difficult task of organizing and often fight and raid one another for short-term gains.
6. The corruption and closed nature of some labor unions has been effectively portrayed by the continual reportage of the corporate-controlled press since the 1970s.
7. Finally, the relative power of capital over labor in the last forty years is also due to the availability of cheap fossil fuel where "for the first (and probably only) time in history, it was cheaper to build a machine to do almost everything than to have a human being do it."[16]

Wisconsin's inspiring worker uprising of 2011 that spread to other states is the latest battlefield in the class war, where the capitalists, under the influence of ALEC-inspired laws, intend to reverse the gains for workers that were established in the New Deal policies of the FDR administration in reaction to the Great Depression of the 1930s.[17] Corporations attempted to exploit the current fiscal crisis by destroying the last major counterweight to their political power—unions. Although unions have traditionally been one of the important sources of financial, grassroots organizational support for the Democratic Party, a class analysis would argue that Democrats and Republicans are two wings of a capitalist party that represent slight variations of the same ruling class. The two parties merely serve to maintain the illusion of choice for the working class.

Working through the newly elected conservative Republicans, corporations followed the disaster capitalism approach outlined by Naomi Klein,[18] where they used a shock created by an emergency—natural or man-made—to impose their preferred policies of privatization, deregulation, and slashing social services to increase their wealth and power, under the guise of reacting to the recession. The new Republican leaders adopted model legislation designed by ALEC—as well as support by the National Chamber of Commerce—to weaken the impact of unions.

Given that capitalism is a global phenomenon, this assault is part of a global struggle, where workers in most countries are also facing massive cuts in jobs, pay, health care, public education, unemployment and retirement benefits, and other social reforms through new demands for austerity.[19]

But why would capitalists want to reduce the buying power of public-sector employees who are potential consumers that will purchase their products? Would not cuts in education and health care diminish the quality of the workforce? These questions overlook the ongoing class war. Because of the current weakness of unions and labor, capitalism has unleashed the full ravages: corporate profit and gain in the short term rather than the maintenance of human needs in the long run. So health, education, fire protection, social security, or any organized sector that can be privatized and turned into a profit-making venture can and will be raided.

A national public reaction inspired by the Wisconsin and Michigan uprisings may lead to some victories for the working class. But these victories are fragile, because even though unions were established and evolved in reaction to capitalism's drive for accumulation, private property, and inequality of rewards, many workers and union leaders, while fighting for their cut, have been transformed from citizens to consumers[20] and became attached to those capitalist values where everything is up for sale.[21] This belief will continue to place them under the power and control of the capitalists/owners and thus help maintain the status quo.[22] The financial and political power of the capitalist class was overtly demonstrated with the 2012 installation of the ALEC-inspired[23] right-to-work law in Michigan,[24] the home of the modern labor movement, where powerful antilabor groups have worked over the years to crush labor.[25]

Some lessons may be gained from the Wisconsin and Michigan uprisings. Lesson one: we must recognize that although it seemed like a sudden attack by the conservative Republican governor and his newly acquired legislative majority, it was the culmination of a longtime class war reacting to FDR's New Deal. Lesson two: the union movement must clean up its own organizational philosophy and reorganize itself. A short list from Harry Kelber, the editor of the *Labor Educator*,[26] argues the following:

- Unions have historically failed to maintain the rights of members to choose their officers in free and fair elections.
- It is difficult to remove top union leaders for incompetence or negligence.
- Union leaders have little direct connection with their members. The leadership is composed of middle-aged to elderly white males who do not depend on the membership for reelection.
- Union leaders, due to their allegiance to the status quo, are timid and passive. They avoid actions like those that built the original labor movement: the sit-down strike in Flint,

Michigan, the civil rights movement sit-ins, continuous picketing at the corporation headquarters, lobbying Capitol Hill, occupying the offices of members of Congress until they eliminate the subsidies, grants, and special favors bestowed on corporations, and fighting against the exportation of jobs to other countries.

Lesson three: we must use the reaction by the workers to conduct what Jane McAlevey described as "whole worker organizing" that

> begins with the recognition that real people do not live two separate lives, one beginning when they arrive at work and punch the clock and another when they punch out at the end of their shift. The pressing concerns that bear down on them every day are not divided into two neat piles, only one of which is of concern to unions. At the end of each shift workers go home, through streets that are sometimes violent, past their kids' crumbling schools, to their often substandard housing, where the tap water is likely unsafe.[27]

In addition, workers need to do the following:

1. Establish community labor centers for developing and maintaining the neighborhood. These must be locations where the community can come together, develop culture, recreate, grow gardens, educate, and organize. These centers will replace the loss of the commons and must be designed so as to capture and develop the interests of families and the young.
2. Educate people about the relationship between the political economy and the environment.[28]
3. Build a political force separate from the existing political

parties (don't rely on the Democratic Party) that brings a progressive voice of labor and community into national, state, and local affairs.

Lesson four: unions must look beyond national boundaries (to be further discussed in chapter 8). The capitalist class has moved beyond the borders through outsourcing and free-trade agreements and inadvertently connected the working class with the world's workers.[29] The working class must increase attempts to join in solidarity with the world's workforce and struggle with the global corporations for better working and living conditions.

Over the years, variations of these solutions have been tried with some success. But new events, unlike any that have happened before in the history of capitalism, are arising that may give the working class new leverage in the class war—the coming age of energy decline—to be discussed in chapter 9.

CHAPTER 8
The International Class Struggle and Globalization

> *The global economy is characterized not only by free trade in goods and services but even more by the free movement of capital ... Given the decisive role that international financial capital plays in the fortunes of individual countries, it is not inappropriate to speak of a global capitalist system.*
>
> —George Soros

> *Where globalization means, as it so often does, that the rich and powerful now have new means to further enrich and empower themselves at the cost of the poorer and weaker, we have a responsibility to protest in the name of universal freedom.*
>
> —Nelson Mandela

This book came out of a question: why in our rich society do so many good, smart, hardworking people who deserve better lives end up in poverty? In order to answer the question, I focused on understanding how capitalism worked. I did this by investigating the struggle between the working class and the capitalist class, primarily in America. But capitalism is a world system,[1] which means that a *global* working class is in struggle with the global capitalist class—so a few words about the larger system.

Although globalization is not a new phenomenon, communities around the globe have been buying from and selling to each other for thousands of years, as early as the time of Marco Polo and the Silk Road.[2] Here, I'm concerned with the effect of global capitalism (beginning in 1800) on the workforce. As capitalism arose out of feudalism, it grew into a new kind of global system, which included the following: (1) northern European countries and the United States, the core economies[3] (those that had a high level of technological development and manufactured complex products); (2) the countries and territories of the rest of the world, the peripheral economies (suppliers of raw materials, agricultural products and cheap labor for the core); and (3) the semiperipheral economies that contained elements of both core and peripherals.

The shift in energy input along with human ingenuity was a key element in the transition from the feudal agrarian economy to our current capitalist global economy. In the feudal economy, energy was locally centered, muscle driven (human and animal), and agrarian (energy from the sun), and since travel was so slow and dangerous and surplus production was insignificant, long trade routes were infrequent. However, everything changed when the energy to drive the new global economy came from minerals: coal and oil that led to the steam engine and internal combustion engine, improving transportation, industry, and agriculture. This new energy was developed and used first in the core countries, led by Britain, and set off the Industrial Revolution.

The history of mineral-based global capitalism developed in three stages. The first stage (1800–1913), with use of coal and oil, led to the Industrial Revolution: the concentration of power, technology, science, and manufacturing in Britain, France, the United States, and Germany.[4] The periphery and semiperiphery included some parts of Europe, most of Asia, Africa, and South America.

The second stage occurred after World War II that left the core countries weakened due to the devastation of two world wars—with the exception of the United States, the sole economic victor. World War I led to the liberation of the colonies from core dominance. World War II led to the exhaustion of England, France, Germany, and Japan and the establishment of the Cold War in which the Soviet Union was in competition with the United States. This was also the time when some peripheral countries took sides in the Cold War, and others strove to become economically independent (e.g., Vietnam in 1945, India in 1947, Kenya in 1963).

The third stage started in the 1980s. The historic impetus of this stage began after World War II, when the wealthy corporate class began to use its influence to counter the welfare state and labor-friendly policies of the FDR administration, with a practice that advocated for free trade, privatization, minimal government intervention in business, the expansion of tax havens, and reduced public expenditure on social services as the best way to conduct our economy. These guiding principles, now called neoliberalism, were intensified in the1980s by the Reagan administration's policies that incorporated[5] the following: (1) cutting taxes on the wealthy and large corporations; (2) reducing government regulations on the environment, worker safety, and product safety; (3) providing billions of dollars in tax incentives and subsidies to transnational corporations; (4) crushing labor unions and keeping the minimum wage low; (5) supporting massive increases in immigration to the United States (further lowering wages for the working class); (6) providing help for American companies in moving their factories to Mexico and China; (7) reducing government support for health care, children, the poor, and the disabled; and (8) working closely with transnational corporations to create "global free trade" and weaken national governments' abilities to manage their economies.

These Reagan policies continued with varying intensity in the administrations of George H. W. Bush, Bill Clinton, George W. Bush, and Barack Obama. These policies gained intellectual legitimacy and provided support for an ideological class war, helped by the economic theories developed at the University of Chicago in the 1950s, where the philosopher-economist Friedrich Hayek and his student Milton Friedman developed a business-oriented, individualistic, market-based philosophy of economics. Under Reagan, this approach inspired the development of an international network of foundations, research institutes, publications, scholars, writers, and public relations organizations to develop, package, and push their ideas and doctrine in order to create the "true story of American greatness." They were quite successful, making it seem as if the free market was the natural condition of humankind and the only possible economic and social order available. Or, as Margaret Thatcher, the leader of the British counterpart of Reagan's policies, also a disciple of Friedrich Hayek, said, "There is no alternative,"—in shorthand, "TINA."

Unlike the positive predictions of the supporters of neoliberalism,[6] its effects for the working class were the following:[7] (1) growing inequality within countries—the rich get richer, the poor get poorer; (2) growing inequality between countries—the core get richer, the periphery get poorer; (3) increasing insecurity among laborers; (4) increasing instability in the economic and financial structures; (5) the influx of commercial values into every sphere of society where market principle trumps humanizing policies;[8] (6) increased domination by corporations; (7) greater threats to climate change and environmental sustainability; (8) increased possibility of armed conflict where the working class becomes the cannon fodder; (9) the creation of a more compliant labor force; (10) massive worldwide pollution; and (11) a core, periphery, semiperiphery instability, where developments in finance, transportation, and technology allowed the production process, that was exclusive to core countries, to move to many emerging countries in the world (the effect of this shift on the United States was the decline of manufacturing, the creation of the rust belt, and the destruction of labor organizations).

An example of a destructive neoliberal program imposed by the World Bank and the IMF (International Monetary Fund)[9] was the

Structural Adjustment Program.[10] Structural adjustment loans were designed to encourage an adjustment of the struggling country's economy by removing government controls and promoting market competition. The outcome of this process often ended when the indebted country was not able to pay back the debt, forcing an opening to exploitative foreign investment that deepened their poverty. Most structural adjustment took place in Latin America and Africa, where the working class ended up paying the costs while their elites and the invading global corporations made all the money.[11] A famous failure of structural adjustment policies was the disaster in Argentina.[12] In the 1990s, Argentina seemed to be a model of successful structural adjustment policies. Foreign investors sent billions of dollars into the country, but in 2001, when the government announced that it could not pay back the borrowed money, the country went into shock, lines formed at banks, government employees received salary reductions, unemployment grew rapidly, and there was an economic meltdown.

Another neoliberal attack on labor came from NAFTA[13] (North American Free Trade Agreement) in 1994 that eliminated restrictions on the flow of goods, services, and investment in North America, pitting workers against one another, lowering wages, and giving corporations more profits. In trying to survive this onslaught, most American workers circled their wagons, focused on their immediate local and national needs, and isolated themselves from international worker movements.

What globalization did to the American working class can be seen by the fact that in 1955, American corporations were staffed with skilled American workers. The largest corporations[14] were General Motors, US Steel, General Electric, Chrysler, and Standard Oil of New Jersey. Currently, the largest corporations are service oriented, staffed by less-skilled and lower-paid labor. The largest corporations are Walmart, the nation's largest employer, Kelly Services (a job placement firm), IBM (a computer hardware and business service company), UPS, McDonald's, and Home Depot. Apple, a "successful"

American corporation, is primarily made up of low-waged laborers from China. The outcome of this shift from manufacturing to service economy was that the US labor force lost jobs, and the remaining employed had lower wages and fewer benefits.

The antiglobalization reaction to the policies of neoliberalism was composed of groups of trade unionists, environmentalists, anarchists, land and indigenous rights activists, human rights organizations, and antisweatshop organizers that defended the poor, the peasants, and the workers. It burst into the headlines in 1999 in the "Battle in Seattle," against the WTO (World Trade Organization),[15] later followed with actions in Prague, Quebec City, Genoa, Barcelona, and Porto Alegre. Antiglobalization had a historical precedent in the uprising of the Zapatista Army of National Liberation in Chiapas, Mexico, on January 1, 1994, reacting to the establishment of NAFTA.

The 2008 financial crisis reenergized the antiglobalization outlook. It took the form in contemporary protests like the Occupy movement that became more concerned for the poor everywhere, the 99 percent who have been disadvantaged by financial globalization. The Arab Spring and the growing unhappiness and push back by the world's workers and poor have led to increased violent reactions against austerity movements in Greece, Spain, Ireland, and Italy. US workers are increasingly involved in antiglobalization actions but not yet effectively coordinated on a worldwide scale.

Workers in the United States will have difficulties in maintaining solidarity with the world's laborers for three major reasons: (1) the power of capitalism, (2) the workers' narrow focus, and (3) the burden of being in the United States.

1. The capitalist ruling class, through its control of governments and laws designed to diminish the power of labor, was able to dominate the workers by creating antilabor policies and taking advantage of the fact that capital is able to move freely across the world, searching for low-cost labor, while

labor, requiring visas or work permits, remained relatively immobile. This led to a situation where corporations received high profits through goods that were manufactured using cheap labor in peripheral economies and then exported to rich core economies. The workers in the United States are vulnerable to losing their hard-won gains when they are in competition with the lower-paid, more desperate laborers in peripheral countries.

2. Because of the isolation of the US working class—as well as the long-established focus on local problems like wages, benefits, work rules, and power that unions have to manage—there have been few attempts to communicate and join in solidarity with the working classes of the world (with some exceptions like USLAW [US Labor Against the War] and IWW).[16] With the ongoing decline in membership, some unions (Teamsters, SEIU, Steelworkers, AFL-CIO)[17] are coming to recognize that they have no futures unless they become global institutions. But globalizing labor has difficulties. US labor has directed some misplaced anger toward workers from other countries that should have been aimed at the actions of the capitalist class. It was US policy that gave incentives to corporations to outsource, as well as the incentives provided by foreign governments and the cheaper labor in other countries. For example, in 1982, at the height of anti-Japanese sentiments, Vincent Chin (who was Chinese) was murdered in Detroit by two white autoworkers that blamed the Japanese for losing their jobs, and currently, many workers in the United States, instead of welcoming and unionizing new allies, are blaming immigrants from other countries for taking their jobs and lowering their wages.

3. As difficult as it has been for the labor force to organize in the United States or interact with worker organizations around the world, it is even more difficult now, because our worker

organizations are viewed as untrustworthy and linked to the arrogant and oppressive policies of the corporate-dominated US government[18] as it seeks ways to maintain its world preeminence through satisfying its profit needs.

Finally, the approaching decline of available cheap energy to sustain capitalism that was partly responsible for the economic collapse of 2008[19] will lead to the eventual decline of globalization, which is vulnerable to high fuel prices, grid breakdowns, political instability, financial problems, disruptions in communications, and increased expenses in manufacturing and transportation.[20] This shift has already begun and is bringing about a defensive response by the capitalist corporations as they seek new ways to maintain profits, and it is the workers and coordinators who are beginning to feel the first effects.

CHAPTER 9

Class Analysis in the Coming Age of Energy Decline

That old oil order is dying, and with its demise we will see the end of cheap and readily accessible petroleum—forever.

—Michael Klare

We are in an environmental crisis because the means by which we use the ecosphere to produce wealth are destructive of the ecosphere itself. The present system of production is self-destructive; the present course of human civilization is suicidal.

—Barry Commoner

So far, we have used the tool of class analysis to understand capitalism and to answer why most people (the working class and the coordinators known as the "middle class" in common parlance and by the media) work hard and mostly remain poor and powerless, while the few (the capitalist class) get rich and powerful. We have also seen how classes are found in different historical stages of society. We saw that class analysis has little to say about hunter-gatherers, who needed no class divisions, as they had little or no surplus and used nature as their grocery store. It was only later, with the coming of agriculture and village life, that there was surplus, divisions of labor, hierarchy, and classes. And later, with the creation of capitalism, the use of steam power, and the adoption of the factory system, we entered the Industrial Revolution, and the creation of even greater surplus and class divisions took the form that we recognize today.

The leaders who first took control of the surplus were the chiefs, the masters, later the lords, kings, and finally, the capitalists. Those who produced the surplus were the peasants, slaves, later the serfs, and ultimately, the wageworkers. This focus on production (manufacturing) and surplus gave us important insights into human history and answered some of the questions that launched me on this journey. The power of this story of production and the weight it gives to labor and human inventiveness furnishes the working class with an identity, an understanding of its place in the class struggle.

What is often overlooked, forgotten, or not stressed enough in the production story is the fact that production is driven by energy.[1] The capture of excess energy supports all the functions of life. Every plant or animal needs energy from food, sunlight, or other sources and must take in more energy than it uses up to survive. Excess energy allows organisms to move, grow, and reproduce. Human societies are dependent on the conversion of energy.[2] Early humans used food based on energy from the sun to provide muscle energy to survive, to forage, to make hunting instruments in order to get high-energy food. They also created clothing from the animal skins to conserve bodily energy that allowed them to move to less-temperate areas. Humans also learned to use fire (energy) to cook meat, strengthen their hunting tools, protect themselves from fierce animals, and drive game from cover. Later, they learned to tame animals and used animal energy to carry produce to market, till their fields, and provide a ready source of protein to add to their diets. In addition to muscle energy, animal energy, and fire, humans also learned to use wind (sails and windmills) and water energy (water-powered mills).

Let's see what happens when we pay more attention to energy in the story of production. Hunter-gatherers slowly depleted the grocery store of nature provided by the energy of the sun. Large animals and easy-to-gather plants were used up, so a new way to acquire food had to be developed. The new way to access energy was found through the taming of plants and animals—the original agricultural revolution (about ten thousand years ago), whose bounty eventually fed a population of one billion by 1800. As agricultural society grew to its energy limits due to soil depletion, timber scarcity, and environmental pollution, Europe faced a dilemma: growing population and diminishing production. Solutions like moving excess population to the New World and to Australia or temporary fixes like importing timber for fuel, using guano (to enrich the soil), and searching for whale oil (used for lamps and candle wax) between the 1750s and 1800s were not sufficient. A new source of energy was needed. The solution again came with human ingenuity—the discovery of a new use of fossil fuels (ancient, stored solar energy). The use of coal began in Britain in the 1700s, followed by the use of oil, discovered in 1859 in Pennsylvania and established as an industry in 1870 with the creation of Standard Oil. This innovation stimulated the Industrial Revolution, leading to steam engines and railroads from 1750 to 1830, electricity, the internal combustion engine, running water, communications, entertainment, and chemicals from 1870 to 1900, and computers, the web, smart machines, and mobile phones from 1960 to present, radically transforming our lives.

The joining together of this new energy source (fossil fuels) with industrialism and the profit-seeking, grow-or-die economy of capitalism on the one hand increased production, wealth, and population (seven billion currently), while on the other hand began to deplete the finite energy base, accelerate environmental destruction and climate change,[3] and create the pollution problems we are currently facing.[4]

The spotlight on energy can give workers a new way to look at their standing. Throughout this book, we focused on capitalism as the producer of goods and services created through human labor and capital, with the help of peripheral energy sources. Now we see that energy in the form of fossil fuels has become the driving force—along with human ingenuity—of economic activities. In fact, if we look back over the last 250 years, we can see how we built our civilization on fossil fuels.[5] Eighty-five percent of our current global economy is driven by fossil fuels.[6] Energy based on fossil fuels is not merely a peripheral contribution to our economy; it is fundamental. But there is danger ahead. Because of the finite nature of fossil fuels and their relationship to economic growth, we are reaching the end of the era of economic expansion,[7] yet our society's infrastructure is based on growth through fossil fuels.

Capitalism with an Energy Focus

If we see energy as being fundamental and problematic, we need to look again at the relationship between energy, capitalism, and the working class. I will use the terms "primary," "secondary," "tertiary," and "catabolic" as conceptual tools to assist us in this task.[8] I'm not rejecting the earlier class analysis definition of capitalism, but I am merely expanding it to illuminate the importance of energy. As we recall, the working-class definition of capitalism recognized that it was a dynamic system that was born and changed, depending on the historic context. Our current energy informed discussion allows for that change: capitalism = primary economy (nature) + secondary economy (production) + tertiary economy (finance). And when capitalism begins to run out of energy and stops growing, it begins to seek profits through consuming itself—it becomes catabolic.[9]

Primary Economy

The primary economy, nature, is the finite aspect of capitalism that the earth provides and humans transform: fish, forests, animals, the biological cycles, soil fertility, pollination, hydrological cycles, the tectonic process that gives us access to metals and minerals, and so on, and finally—most important for our current purpose—fossil fuels.

Secondary Economy

The secondary economy focuses on production. Throughout this book, it was defined as capitalism, a "socioeconomic system where social relations [human relations] are based on commodities for exchange, private ownership of production, and on the exploitation of wage labor," which requires growth to survive: more manufacturing, more trade, more transport, and more energy.

Tertiary Economy

The tertiary economy is the rapidly growing financial economy whose job is to "grease the wheels" of the primary and secondary economies—to manage money in order to maximize return on invested capital. It is composed of banks, insurance companies, mortgage companies, advertisers, legal institutions, and investment institutions. It has recently become newsworthy due to the development of creative abstractions like hedge funds and credit default swaps and the corporate-dominated government policies that allowed the stock market to be turned into an unregulated casino. The relationship between the decline of energy and production in the primary and secondary economies, as well as the collapse of the tertiary economy that depended on permanent growth, was partly responsible for the economic crisis of 2008[10] (see appendix 2). That crisis gave rise to the beginning of a new formation of capitalism—the catabolic phase.[11]

Catabolic Capitalism

The term "catabolic capitalism" refers to the point where capitalism is in crisis and doesn't have access to cheap energy necessary for maintaining growth and profits, so it begins to eat itself by

> confiscating and selling off the stranded assets of the bankrupt productive and public sectors, dodging or dismantling legalities and regulations

while pocketing taxpayer subsidies, hoarding scarce resources and peddling arms to those fighting over them, and preying upon the utter desperation of people who can no longer find gainful employment elsewhere.[12]

The working class will be its first course with increased unemployment, destruction of unions, decline of wages, and loss of benefits (all currently happening). With the increasing expense of fossil fuels, the remaining employees will eventually be forced to replace the fossil fuel operated machines and smart technology with their own energy, most likely under serf-like conditions. If this transition occurs, it will lead to the breakdown of the infrastructure, shortages, chaos, starvation, plagues, political upheaval, and ruthless capitalist control over the remaining declining industrial base.

A Short History: From Production to Catabolic Capitalism

Twenty years prior to the oil crisis of 1973, the balance between the primary, secondary, and tertiary economies (energy, production, and banking) seemed to work well (as least for a portion of our white male population). One reason was that in the nineteenth and twentieth centuries, the United States was the number-one oil producer in the world; currently, it's the third largest. Because of this advantage, the United States "floated to victory in two world wars on a sea of oil."[13] For example, if you look to World War II from the oil perspective, you will see that the United States was able to produce an overwhelming amount of military supplies to support our allies due to its oil-based energy capacities. The attack on Pearl Harbor was an attempt to temporarily cripple the US fleet so that the Japanese Empire could hold on to oil centers in the Dutch East Indies. The bloody victory of the Soviet Union over the Nazis in Stalingrad, a turning point in the war, occurred when the oil-starved Nazis needed to get to the Baku oil fields. And finally the

Desert Fox, Erwin Rommel, was defeated when his oil supplies were stopped. Looking at recent history through an oil lens can give us new insights into why the world changed the way it did, as well as some of our current problems.

The United States' energy advantage furnished the illusion that the American dream was possible: seemingly unlimited fossil fuels fed an ever-expanding secondary economy, and wages were increasing. The United States was the sole economic survivor after World War II and was thus able to profit through "saving" Europe through the Marshall Plan and Japan through General Douglas MacArthur's Supreme Commander Allied Powers administration, or SCAP.

But since the 1970s, US economic power was successfully challenged by (1) increased competition from Europe and Japan; (2) the loss of its oil advantage due to the arrival of peak oil (that point when the production of oil reaches its maximum rate, after which production will gradually level off toward a long-term decline [see glossary]) and competition from other oil producers;[14] and (3) the oil embargo in 1973 by OPEC (the Organization of the Petroleum Exporting Countries). These conditions challenged the assumption that cheap energy would be available for the growth of the secondary economy. This assumption of growth is crucial to the ongoing reign of capitalism, since growth was the way capitalism overcame its many crises over the years.[15]

In order to maintain profits, US-based international corporations lobbied the government to be free from tariffs, promote unrestricted trade, to outsource labor, and globalize.[16] They relied on improvements in transportation, information technology, and military capacity while outsourcing[17] labor and industry and exploiting the natural wealth and lower costs of labor and lack of environmental regulations of countries they could control. Industry in America was shipped overseas, the rust belt (the declining industry of some cities in the Northeast and Midwest characterized by aging factories and a falling population) was created, wages were reduced, and unemployment increased. The American labor force was weakened, and many of the remaining worker organizations were undermined, destroyed, or corrupted by the owners of industries.[18]

The United States became a world power in the era of cheap oil. Our infrastructure grew by depending on fossil fuels more than did other countries, so when we run out, our fall will probably be greater.[19] An excellent example of the catabolic process, where capitalism keeps profiting from social decline, is what is happening to Detroit, Michigan—Motor City. In the 1960s, Detroit was one of America's wealthiest cities with a population of two million. Now it is the epicenter of American decline, losing more than one million inhabitants (according to the 2010 census). It was a victim of outsourcing—reducing labor costs in order to maintain profits by moving to areas that had cheaper labor costs. But outsourcing has an effect: the "insourcing" of heartbreaking stories of the unemployed, the loss of family ties, housing, education, social services, transportation, health care, and so on—what is currently happening to America and the rest of the industrial world[20] and responded to by the ruling class through "austerity,"[21] a new name for the class war against workers.

The Energy Problems for the Working Class: Addiction and Finitude

The energy that oil provided allowed industrial society to grow so rapidly that it placed the population in a vulnerable situation. Richard Heinberg described the first part of this problem—addiction:

> The industrial revolution, still continuing, is all about replacing human and animal labor with the work of machines running directly or indirectly on fossil energy. Each day, the energy from oil used by people around the world equals the work of some 180 billion humans. It is as if the average global

| *Seeing Through The System* |

man, woman or child had 30 slaves toiling around the clock. But those petroleum "ghost slaves" are not evenly distributed. Each of us in the U.S. has, on average, more than 120 of them. This is the energetic basis of our American Way of Life.

We have become overly dependent on fossil fuels to conduct our daily lives.[22]

Michael Klare points to the second part of this problem—finitude:

> To put the matter baldly: the world economy requires an increasing supply of affordable petroleum. The Middle East alone can provide that supply. That's why Western governments have long supported "stable" authoritarian regimes throughout the region, regularly supplying and training their security forces. Now, this stultifying, petrified order, whose greatest success was producing oil for the world economy, is disintegrating. Don't count on any new order (or disorder) to deliver enough cheap oil to preserve the Petroleum Age.[23]

There is not enough oil to allow us to maintain our profit-seeking, growth-oriented economy. So unless we change the system, guess what class will replace Heinberg's "energy ghost slaves" as energy becomes more expensive and difficult to find and labor is abundant and cheap? And don't expect there will be a resurgence of good jobs for the working class, because the energy required for industrial growth will not be available, so the workforce will become slaves to a system that is in decline and eating itself to maintain profits (remember Detroit).

The attempt to maintain growth by burning declining fossil fuels is also leading to the destruction of our climate, a reality not yet publicly accepted by most corporations and politicians. They are making too much money by ignoring or hiding it, but the scientists are in agreement about the danger.[24] A few economists are breaking away from the traditional growth paradigm held by most mainstream economists. They recognize the importance and effects of energy decline.[25] Only a few worker organizations have yet recognized the implications of energy decline and climate change[26] for the working class. Why did it take so long to see this problem, and why do some still not see it?

1. We have grown up in an economy dependent on fossil fuels, and we think it is natural; we are like fish in water. As Marshall McLuhan said, "We don't know who discovered water, but we know it wasn't the fish."
2. We were amazed by our achievements and convinced ourselves that new ideas and technology could solve any problems, causing us to overlook the destructive impact our modern discoveries were already having on the life support systems of our planet.
3. Those in power are making too much money, so they resist change; remember Upton Sinclair's statement: "It is difficult to get a man to understand something when his salary depends on his not understanding it."
4. Because of the influence of capitalism that depends on continual growth, markets, and the separation of workers from nature, we have not been able to experience or think of the benefits of a symbiotic (mutually beneficial) relationship with nature.
5. We thought that our civilization was an exception to the earlier civilizations that fell: the Roman Empire, Mayan, Spanish, Ottoman, British, Easter Island, and so on.
6. We experience fear, as expressed in Jean Baudrillard's description of Las Vegas: "The skylines lit up at dead of night, the air-conditioning systems cooling empty hotels

in the desert and artificial light in the middle of the day all have something both demented and admirable about them. The mindless luxury of a rich civilization, and yet of a civilization perhaps as scared to see the lights go out as was the hunter in his primitive night."[27]

7. We are trapped within the mind-set of capitalism, which, through its propaganda industry, privatizes our consciousness,[28] and guides us into an isolating, predatory, commodity-centered concern that makes it easy to disregard the community or group. This mind-set generally ignores history, the larger context, or the future.

The Danger of Denial: Complexity and EROEI (Energy Returned on Energy Invested)

We are at a crucial point in history, more dangerous than the devastation of earlier civilizations that fell due to deforestation, soil erosion/depletion, ineffective water management, overhunting, overfishing, or overpopulation. Now, in addition to those earlier problems, we are facing human-caused climate change, toxin buildup, and energy shortages, all accelerated by the fossil-fuel-energy-dependent, constantly growing, and more complex global capitalist system.

In *The Collapse of Complex Societies*, Joseph Tainter[29] argued that excessive complexity is the best explanation for the collapse of civilizations. As societies develop, the energy and resource costs for complexity initially provide greater benefits, making life easier. Eventually these benefits from increasing complexity became more expensive relative to the costs. So there comes a point when all the energy and resources available to a society are required just to maintain the level of complexity for that society, at which point the society has lessened its ability to withstand stress and is vulnerable to collapse. One of Tainter's examples is the decline of the Roman Empire. As Roman agricultural output slowly declined and population increased, per-capita energy availability dropped. The Romans solved this problem by conquering outsiders and seizing their energy surpluses (grain, slaves, etc.). But as the empire grew, so did the cost of maintaining communications, the military, and local government. Eventually, the increasing costs of conquering for more territory that was less able to benefit the empire drained the Roman treasury, so it could not resolve new problems like invasions, rebellions, or crop failures.

The United States is following the same path as the Roman Empire. We are reaching the point where problems that arise cannot be solved through increased growth and complexity, since the economy is contracting. In order to maintain its energy needs and stem the contraction, the capitalist ruling class will continue to increase military spending, develop a security state, make new laws to criminalize rebellion, and conduct oil and resource wars. Lower on the list will be spending on health, education, and jobs for infrastructure repair (sewers, water, roads, canals, bridges, utilities). But, as in the Roman example, we are also continually being confronted with costs of new wars and catastrophes[30] (e.g., Iraq, Afghanistan, the Arab Spring, the Deepwater Horizon oil spill, Hurricane Katrina,[31] the 2012 Midwest drought and wildfires, superstorm Hurricane Sandy, and the continuing world economic crisis). We will eventually approach the point where our industrial civilization cannot afford to maintain its own existence. You can see evidence of this now in the deterioration of our cities and towns,[32] our educational system, and our health care system and the loss of public commons.[33]

If we look to petroleum extraction with the above complexity argument in mind, we can see that at first, oil was easily gotten, almost like sticking a straw in the earth. This ease encouraged the development of an infrastructure based on oil. But as the initial easy-to-get oil became more difficult to access, complexity entered the picture. In order to get more oil to feed the infrastructure, new and more expensive ways were devised: deeper drilling sites, drilling in hard-to-access land, ocean-based drilling (by 2020, it is estimated that 50 percent of world oil production will be offshore),[34] mining oil shale, and tar sand mining. Added to the costs of military control and conquest of oil rich lands, these new developments are more complex, expensive (ultimately paid for by taxpayers), require more energy to produce per unit of oil, and create massive amounts of pollution.[35]

A finite amount of oil is available to the world economies, and it is becoming more expensive to extract. Oil analysts[36] have a name for this condition—EROEI: energy returned on energy invested. Energy produced / energy used = EROEI. For example, if oil is selling for $200 per barrel and it costs $20 in energy to produce a barrel, the EROEI is 10:1. In its early days, oil frequently yielded an EROEI greater than 100:1, where 1 percent or less of the energy contained in a barrel of oil had to be used to deliver a barrel of oil. Oil development is currently considered to have an EROEI of about 15:1 and declining. The higher the EROEI number, the better for oil company profits. When EROEI is equal to one (1:1), it means that the energy extracted is equal to the energy invested, so it is too expensive to use as an energy source. The tar sand deposits in Canada have an EROEI of 7:1 for extraction, but this drops to 3:1 after it has been upgraded and refined into gasoline.[37] The EROEI of around 5:1 is considered to be the minimum required to sustain an industrial society.[38] In addition to being more expensive, this process generates multiple times more greenhouse gases than does the production of conventional oil and pollutes massive amounts of water needed for the process.[39]

Recently, the IEA (International Energy Agency) pointed out that by 2020, US oil output would surpass that of Saudi Arabia, making the United States self-reliant and an oil exporter.[40] News of energy independence is based on shale oil extraction technology that has let loose an energy boom in the United States and has created new jobs and driven down the price of oil and natural gas. This news ignores the EROEI aspect—that the new oil and natural gas will cost more, economically and environmentally. In fact, according to the US National Center for Atmospheric Research, switching from coal to gas increases global warming.[41] Pursuing this technology will also end in increased competition for water resources needed for the energy extraction, leading to peak water. In addition, oil demand by China and India is expected to continue growing. The news by the IEA must be balanced by the fact that oil is a finite resource.[42]

Many reacting to the end of cheap oil and economic growth argue that fossil fuels can be substituted by alternative energies: wind, tidal, solar, hydrogen, geothermal, and so on or by technological innovations. But unless the population intervenes powerfully, once we enter a decline in fossil fuel availability, our growth-based economy will seek to maintain its profits. The easiest way to do this is by increasing the exploitation of the working class and destroying the social safety net. Fuel prices will probably decline in the short-term but rise in the long-term. Individuals and nations will react by hoarding, leading to energy shortages and wars. The fight for the remaining fossil fuels will overshadow the demand for a new energy infrastructure based on non–fossil fuel solutions, which must face the reality that the construction of a new infrastructure requires not just money but energy. And that's the very commodity coming into short supply. There are no current substitutes for the efficiency and portability of fossil fuels and the power of the industries that endorse them. "Alternative energies will never replace fossil fuels at the scale, rate and manner at which the world currently consumes them, and humankind's ingenuity will simply not overcome the upper limits of geology & physics."[43]

What Is the Working Class to Do?

There is a time ... when the operation of the machine becomes so odious, makes you so sick at heart, that you can't take part. You can't even passively take part! And

> *you've got to put your bodies upon the gears and upon the wheels, upon the levers, upon all the apparatus, and you've got to make it stop! And you've got to indicate to the people who run it, to the people who own it—that unless you're free, the machine will be prevented from working at all!*
>
> —Mario Savio

> *Don't waste any time mourning—organize!*
>
> —Joe Hill

The working class is confronted with three problems: (1) mainstream society, which includes most workers, is unwilling to acknowledge the reality of ecological destruction, energy finiteness, and climate change; (2) in the long term, we must be prepared to live in a world with lower levels of available energy; and (3) the US working class is currently not self-aware or organized as a class. True, some craft, industrial, and government unions and worker organizations are putting up a fight, but the ruling class is currently winning. Of course, this may change as the current economic crisis begins to anger more employees and wildcat strikes begin.

Most supporters of the working class who recognize this state of affairs suggest variations of the above messages given by Mario Savio and Joe Hill. But stopping the system and organizing requires that we identify as a group and agree to a set of goals. That is not the case currently. Although there is not much time left to diminish the extent of the coming catastrophe, no other group is ready or able to struggle effectively with the capitalist class.

There is some hope though, through the inspiration of the Occupy / 99 Percent movement. In a short time, the 99 Percent movement has done what the working class has been unable to do since the struggles right after World War II. The 99 Percent have named the enemy and gotten a significant portion of the public to symbolically identify the current power holders as the 1 percent. But this is only the beginning. The 99 Percent gives us a useful frame of the struggle, but details are yet to be developed.

The message of the 99 Percent is similar to the message of the working class: a small group of capitalists versus the many. The working class must join with the 99 Percent, organize, and educate itself. Following are a few of the many attempts to solve the problem of energy decline and environmental catastrophe that the working class may learn from. First, a warning! Economic conditions don't necessarily mean that consciousness and actions will follow. History has informed us that most working-class aggressiveness has come when there was an upsurge in the economy that gave the working class new hope.[44]

    a. Cuba[45]—which lost access to cheap oil in the 1990s when its source, the Soviet Union, collapsed—was forced to immediately change from a petrochemical industrial method of farming to a local, labor-intensive, organic mode of production.

    b. Judi Bari transformed the organization Earth First! from a conservation movement to a social movement through a series of political actions to unite workers and environmentalists in pursuit of sustainable forestry practices against multinational logging corporations[46] in Northern California's redwood forests.

    c. Since the mid-1980s, community supported agriculture, also known as subscription farming, has been growing in the United States. CSA is a partnership between farms and communities that provides a direct link between the production and consumption of food.[47]

    d. The transition town movement has been created—"An international grassroots effort to harness the collective genius of ordinary people to find solutions to the serious challenges of climate change, peak oil and economic instability."[48]

| *Seeing Through The System* |

e. The Rebuild the Dream movement is uniting progressives to find green solutions for fixing our economy.[49]
f. The New Economy Movement[50] is a movement to bring together organizations, projects, theorists, activists, and ordinary citizens whose agenda is to rebuild the American political economy from the bottom up. This is with the larger goal of "democratized ownership of the economy for the '99 percent' in an ecologically sustainable and participatory community-building fashion."[51]
g. The Political Economy Research Institute advocates for a green full-employment economy[52] that addresses the problem of climate change, efficiency, renewable energy, and investing in a green economy.
h. The NELP (National Employment Law Project) has developed programs to train workers to put into action the "green" retrofitting of buildings. It is a program supported by labor, environmentalist, and commercial building owners, focused on Los Angeles, Seattle, and Milwaukee.[53]
i. The California State Grange's[54] Green Grange program supports small family farmers and promotes sustainable organic agriculture.
j. Public Citizen,[55] organized by Ralph Nader, serves as the voice of the people in the nation's capital, whose goal is to "ensure that all citizens are represented in the halls of power."
k. The US Federation of Worker Cooperatives,[56] founded in 2004, is an organization that supports the growth and development of worker cooperatives through educational outreach, conferences and events, resource referrals, and networking and training opportunities.
l. Three recent excellent resources that deal with the problem of the system and democracy that contain good

information and access to resources are: *What Then Must We do?: Straight Talk About the Next American Revolution* by Gar Alperovitz, *Democracy at Work: A Cure for Capitalism* by Rick Wolff, and *Yes* Magazine's Spring 2013 issue "How Cooperatives Are Driving the New Economy."

In addition to these models, there is a shift toward ecological and community awareness among the young, educators, neighborhoods, municipalities, politicians, the media, and investors in the stock market, as well as some businesses. The environmentalist Paul Hawken argues that this ecological shift is the largest mass movement in the world today.[57] The working class that has traditionally focused on equity issues now needs to join with and support this new mass movement and share its experiences of worker-owned cooperatives like Mondragon[58] in Spain and the Green Worker Cooperative in the United States.[59]

Capitalism has oriented us to wish for a society that needs energy to produce commodities that we purchase to give us more comfortable lives and make us happy. This approach actually destroys our relationships with one another and the earth. It turns us, for the most part, into isolated competing consumers and wage slaves wedded to a system that creates false needs, inequality, and pollution. To overcome this condition, workers must struggle to recognize the importance of solidarity with one another and the earth.

It is also useful to learn from the triumphs and mistakes of our predecessors. In 1976, Barry Commoner summed up the problem when he argued that the production of profit was the major cause of environmental destruction.[60] He spoke out for the most common victims of environmental pollution when he stated that cause of the crisis was not how humans interact with nature but in how they interact with one another. Solving the environmental crisis requires that we solve poverty, racial injustice, and war.

In order to proceed with an attempt to change the system, Commoner

1. was instrumental in creating a way to communicate technical information so that the public could be involved;
2. organized campaigns against nuclear testing, chemical pollution, and environmental decay;
3. promoted the "precautionary principle" that new chemicals and technologies should be approved only after they are demonstrated to be safe;
4. took part in many grassroots environmental campaigns;
5. repeatedly communicated with the victims of pollution: the poor, minorities, and working-class communities;
6. exposed the role of capitalism and profit;
7. developed the four laws of ecology: (1) everything is connected; (2) everything must go somewhere; (3) nature knows best; and (4) there is no such thing as a free lunch.
8. Started a political campaign and formed a new party—Citizens Party—that linked environmental issues to social/political issues; and
9. ran for president in 1980 but received less than one-third of 1 percent of the vote.

Barry Commoner was effective and truly deserves Ralph Nader's praise as the "greatest environmentalist of the twentieth century," but the system was not brought down. The power of the petrochemical industry and their media, combined with the belief by many environmentalists that green capitalism was the solution, drowned out Commoner's arguments. Perhaps the public wasn't ready, perhaps the situations were not historically ideal, given that most working-class struggles have come at a time of economic growth that drove workers to higher aspirations,[61] perhaps Commoner's forces were not organized well enough or didn't understand capitalism, perhaps, perhaps, perhaps. These are issues that we must struggle with.

The working class must be careful to use a strategy that will not exclude them from the political process. In competing with the vast power of the status quo, supported by the corporate media, workers need to focus on issues or projects that touch the immediate concerns of the majority. In the short run, workers must ally with the forces of reform, while in the long term educate themselves, develop allies, and grow a movement that will keep focus on the goals of a sustainable, just society as it engages in political struggle against the capitalist-inspired military- petroleum complex that only has profit for the few as its goal. According to Bill McKibben, it is a rogue industry, "reckless like no other force on Earth. It is Public Enemy Number One to the survival of our planetary civilization."[62]

If the working people, the largest and potentially most powerful force in the world, join with the movements that promote ecological awareness, sustainability, and social justice, they can help create a softer landing in the escape from the fossil fuel trap that our corporate-controlled economy has led us into. In an earlier era, the rallying call was "Workers of the world unite for you have nothing to lose but your chains," and now it may be "Workers, social justice activists, and environmentalists of the earth unite—the future of our planet is at stake!"

APPENDIX 1
Social Class Questionnaire (complete)

Please respond to the following questions about social class. Before answering, talk to colleagues, friends, and family about your responses. Some people who answered felt sad because they uncovered painful family secrets; some said they saw the world and their relationships with friends and family differently. Some even said that these questions brought up issues that forced them to reframe their lives. In any event, by focusing on answers to these questions, you will probably trigger[1] memories of events in your life that you've forgotten about that can make a difference in the way you look at your world today. You may also find that many of the following questions are excellent dialogue starters for family gatherings, card nights, or any social functions.

1. What is your own work history? What kinds of jobs have you held? What skills have you developed? Which jobs did you like best? Why? What jobs did you hate? Why?

2. What is your dominant image when you think of workers?

3. What work did your grandparents do? What work did your parents do? Did immigration affect this work history? If so, how? Was there a big difference in occupations between the generations? If so, how

were you aware of that difference? Based on this work history, what were your own expectations about the work you would do?

4. What were the stated and unstated assumptions about work in your family? How was work viewed? Was it ever talked about? As a child, did you have any understanding of your parents' work lives? If not, why do you think that was, and how do you think it might have shaped your own attitudes toward work?

5. How did your parents' work affect family patterns? Did it have an impact on who ate together? When you ate? What time the family spent together? Were your parents emotionally and physically exhausted or unavailable because of their work situations? If your parents' work had been different, how would it have changed your life?

6. What did the parents of your friends do? Did you feel differently about their work than you did about that of your parents? What sense of pride or shame did you have about your parents' work? Has it changed as you have grown older? If it has changed, what brought about the change?

7. Pick five values, expectations, or orientations that seem to be most valued in your family. Then pick five that seem to be least valued or important.

Getting by; making a moderate living; making a very good living; gaining social status or prominence; open communication among family members; going to a place of worship; keeping up with the neighbors; being physically fit or athletic; working out psychological issues through therapy; helping others; getting married and having children; respecting law and order; defending one's country; staying out of trouble with the law; being politically or socially aware; recognition; community service; saving money; making your money work for you; enjoying your money; getting a high school degree; getting a college degree; getting an advanced or professional degree; learning a trade; helping to advance the cause of one's racial, religious, or cultural group; physical appearance; being a professional; being an entrepreneur; owing a home; being patriotic; going to private school; not being wasteful; having good etiquette. Others:

8. Who does most of the work in your household (remember to also include washing clothes, cooking dinners, raising the children)?

9. How would you characterize the socioeconomic nature of the neighborhood(s) you grew up in? Of the larger community you grew up in?

10. How would you characterize your family's socioeconomic background? (For example: poor, working class, lower middle class, middle class, upper middle class, ruling class.) What tells you this?

11. Think of one or two people who you perceive to be from a different social class from you (someone from high school, from a job, from a club). What class would you say they belong to? What tells you this? Besides money, what do you see as distinguishing them from you (or your family from their families)? How would you characterize their values or their families' values? How are they the same or different from yours?

12. If money were not an issue, what work would you most want to do? Why? (The purpose of this question is to query if most of us are doing what we really want to do in this society.)

13. What do you appreciate? Have you gained from your class background experience?

14. What has been hard for you being from your class background?

15. What would you never like to hear said about people from your class background?

16. What impact does your class background have on your current attitudes, behaviors, and feelings (about money, work, relationships with people from the same class / from a different class, your sense of self, expectations about life, your politics, etc.)?

APPENDIX 2
The Working Class and the Current Crisis of Capitalism

The one and only responsibility of business is to make as much money for the stockholders as possible—the doctrine of social responsibility [for business] is a fundamentally subversive doctrine in a free society.

—Milton Friedman

The top 1 percent have the best houses, the best educations, the best doctors, and the best lifestyles.

—Joseph Stiglitz

In *The Shock Doctrine: The Rise of Disaster Capitalism*, Naomi Klein pointed out that the shock from disasters like the war in Iraq, the tsunami in Asia, and Hurricane Katrina permitted multinational corporations to implement corporate-friendly policies that disadvantaged the local common working people. For example, after the tsunami in Sri Lanka, capitalists,[1] in the name of freedom and the free market, were able to place a luxury resort where there used to be a fishing village. After Hurricane Katrina, capitalists moved to expel many poor black residents, privatize and commercialize public schools, and get rid of teacher unions.

Why not apply Klein's perspective to the economic crisis of 2008?

We might think of it as a way for capitalism to take advantage of a financial tsunami that it caused. Through the chaos of that disaster, capitalists could protect and maintain themselves and increase their power by
- ramping up their media to create more fear and obedience among the citizens;
- getting rid of unprofitable investments (useless factories, obsolete equipment, bad financial agreements, out-of-date commodities, redundant workers, etc.);
- increasing the transfer of wealth from the working class to the capitalists through changing taxes, laws, regulations, lobbying, and controlling the actions of governmental institutions;
- maintaining for-profit health care, denying the possibility of single payer;
- protecting the wealth and interests of the financial oligarchy by solidifying and consolidating the remaining institutions that control our economy (banks, investment and mortgage institutions);
- increasing the military and prison budget under the pretext of promoting security;
- increasing the spying on citizens by using security concerns to control dissent;
- weakening and privatizing public education and destroying teacher unions;
- privatizing public spaces, shifting public services to private for-profit services, attempting to get rid of social security, pension funds, and so on;
- attacking the power of public and private-sector workers to organize through unions; and
- controlling the minds of the population with selective reporting by corporate-controlled media, diverting attention to irrelevant stories about celebrities, sex, violence, fear, passive, mind-deadening entertainment, and sports or only

giving the capitalists' side of the story and placing much of the blame for the crisis on the working class, especially people of color and immigrants.

All this is accomplished by the capitalists while hiding under the veneer of an anemic attempt by the Obama administration trying to protect and copy FDR's New Deal policies used to combat the Great Depression of the 1930s. Obama's current program pretends to give hope that lives will return to normal through the development of green industries, a stimulation program to restabilize our financial institutions, a new health care plan that maintains the profit motive, "shovel ready" projects to employ workers, increased support for the unemployed, and rescuing the "middle class" but in no way corrects the structurally imposed dehumanizing economic inequality that capitalism enforces and the periodic crises and environmental catastrophe that it causes.

The task of a class analysis is to use an inspection of this crisis to help us better understand how capitalism creates the great disparities in wealth and power that the capitalist class has over the working class and how, with this knowledge, we can begin to transform the economy into one that benefits and respects all humans as well as the environment.

A reminder before we begin.

How we reflect on the world consists in good part on the concepts we choose. Concepts are like flashlights—they call our attention to some aspects of reality while leaving others in shadows. For example, working-class analysis describes its members as workers, while the capitalists describe them as replaceable costs of production. Class itself is also a concept central to the working class worldview, while it is not a concern of the capitalists. (Unfortunately, too many workers have been trained to think like capitalists.)

In order to clarify the crisis, I will describe capitalism as a system that contains three subsystems that interact with one another in a tenuous balance: the primary economy (what the earth and sun provide), the secondary economy (what is commonly known as capitalism), and the tertiary economy (the financial domain). In the following story of the crisis, I will first describe the secondary economy and then tell the crisis story and show how the tertiary economy grew. Then I will enhance the story of the crisis with the generally unacknowledged impact of the primary economy. This explanation is a working-class analysis that represents the condition and not necessarily the consciousness of the vast majority of the population.

So let's begin our class analysis of capitalism.

The System—Capitalism (The Secondary Economy)

The basic law of capitalism is you or I, not both you and I.

—Karl Liebknecht

The traditional definition of economics as being the production of goods and services—that most of our understanding of class is based upon—will now be described as the secondary economy that operated effectively from the time that the United States industrialized until the 1970s, for about 150 years (1820–1970). At this time, attention was focused on the secondary economy, the profit machine of capitalism. It was facilitated by the primary and tertiary economies. After the '70s, the tertiary economy and primary economy exerted new pressures on the secondary economy that assisted in amplifying the 2008 crisis.

- We live within the capitalist economic system where most people engaged in economic activity fall into one of two groups: (1) capitalists and their managers, who own or manage the industries, corporations, and businesses; and (2)

workers, who only own their power to labor—their ability to work.
- Capitalism is based the following premises:
  a. private property rights and the private ownership of businesses
  b. the market, where exchange of commodities occurs
  c. the separation of ownership and work (capitalist/boss versus worker)
  d. the profit motive
  e. the necessity for growth
  f. the availability of cheap fossil fuels and other natural resources that make the secondary economy possible (more about that when I discuss the primary economy)
- Class analysis recognizes capitalism as a system where society's material needs are satisfied primarily through exchange in the market. In that practice, the working class is turned into a commodity by selling its labor power to capitalists who own the factories, businesses, and corporations. These owners give workers back a portion of the value they create, through the wage system, and use the rest, the surplus, to grow their holdings, for if they don't grow, competitors will swallow them up.
- A capitalist is able to pay workers less than the value of labor power because, thanks to the premise of private property, the capitalists own the jobs, the buildings, machines and equipment, and energy sources without which the labor force cannot work. Workers only own their labor power, and they must compete for jobs with each other. Those that lose become the unemployed, a kind of reserve army of potential employees that keeps the labor force worried and their pay low.
- These days, working for wages seems natural, where the capitalist buys labor at a "fair price," but with investigation,

we see that this transaction hides the fact that workers must rent out parts of themselves to the bosses who do with them what they wish, turning workers into things (commodities) and dehumanizing them. In addition, the working class creates more value than it is recompensed for—it is exploited.

- To be effective, capitalists must constantly find ways to cheapen the cost of production and sell more than competing capitalists. The best way to cheapen the cost of production is to use fewer employees: to replace workers with machines, computers, and robots or to find a cheaper labor force in other countries.
- As profits decline, the capitalists try to recover by using machines that save labor and cut costs in order to get ahead of their competitors. But competing capitalists are doing the same thing, so the profit continues to fall to the point where production is not profitable. At the same time, consumption declines as workers that are displaced don't have an adequate income to buy the many commodities that are filling the retailers' shelves.
- Because of the excess of products that must be dumped onto the market, smaller capitalists, who have less financial reserves, go out of business or are absorbed by their competitors who grow larger, while workers lose their jobs.
- The remaining employees who didn't lose their jobs to machines receive lower wages from the bigger capitalists, who also, at cheaper rates, purchase the dumped machines of their defeated competition.
- This cycle of crisis and renewal serves to strengthen and expand a capitalism that contains fewer but larger corporations. Thus we see that, as Naomi Klein stated, crisis (or the business slump or recession) is the way that capitalism functions. For in each crisis, the bigger firms absorb the smaller ones. In later crises, when bigger industries fail, the

crisis becomes greater, until today, where many say that some financial corporations are "too big to fail," so the government (the taxpayers) must save them.
- Given that capitalism requires growth and profit, it has developed other practices to get rid of its overproduction. The working class is encouraged to purchase more, promoting the development of advertising, debt, and the consumer culture. But there are even other ways: create new commodities, find markets in other countries, and sell commodities that need to be periodically replaced—known as planned or perceived obsolescence.[2]
- But even those techniques have not solved the problem of overproduction, so capitalism has come to (1) shift its funds out of reinvestments in plants, equipment, and the labor force and move to financial assets that can generate their own expansion (at least temporarily); and (2) depend on industries that rely on a spiral of creation-destruction-creation. The best example is the weapons industry that creates commodities that destroy commodities or are themselves destroyed, thus requiring new replacement commodities.[3]
- The ultimate method that capitalism uses to destroy excessive commodities and industries in order to rebuild itself is war. You may call war the ultimate stimulus package. Think of how the United States reached its industrial golden age right after Word War II, where we increased corporate profits through rebuilding the destroyed infrastructures of Europe and Japan. In his documentary *South of the Border*, Oliver Stone spoke with Argentina's former president Néstor Kirchner who stated, in an earlier discussion with former president George W. Bush, that when he (Kirchner) suggested that South America needed a new Marshall Plan, referring to the World War II–era European reconstruction plan, Bush suggested that "the best way to revitalize the economy is war" and that the United States has grown

stronger with war.[4] (While you digest this, think of the millions of families—Korean, Vietnamese, Iraqi, Afghan, Nicaraguan, American, and others—whose lives have been devastated by war, and then contrast that pain to the profits gained by corporations, such as Bechtel, Halliburton, Aegis Defense Services, Custer Battles, General Dynamics, Chevron, ExxonMobil, etc.).[5]

How This Crisis Happened

- Between the 1950s and 1970s, the economy of the United States, the only standing economy after World War II, was the envy of the world. This was due to the postwar boom of rising production, wages, and consumption. The wage increases were due to a history of labor shortages that forced capitalists to compete for workers, spurring the immigration of the previous century.
- Much of the world viewed American capitalism as the ideal. The returning soldiers received the GI bill, became educated, bought houses, cars, and appliances, gained status, and entered the "middle class." Many of the women, who were working during the war, lost their jobs to the returning men, but since one wage earner could then support a family and feminism had not yet become a political force, this was not seen as a problem. This boon had little effect on people of color and immigrants who were still relegated to the bottom of the economy.
- This was also the time where the Marshall Plan, a program of economic aid for the reconstruction of Europe (1948–1952), was implemented. It seemed to reflect the "good heart of America," but actually, American capitalists believed that poor countries were more likely to become communist, and they didn't want that to happen, for it would hinder the growth of a capitalist market.

- In the early 1970s, the postwar boom ended. Rick Wolff, a University of Massachusetts Amherst economist, explains what happened after this period with a chart that came from a lecture titled "Capitalism Hits the Fan."[6]
- This chart illustrates the steady growth of worker productivity, workers' wages, and capitalist profits from 1890 until today. It also reveals that workers' wages flattened out in mid 1970s while the capitalists' profits soared.
- By the early '70s, the injured and devastated societies of World War II (France, Germany, Great Britain, Japan) had rebuilt themselves and began to successfully compete with US capitalism—they were eventually able to take away much of our secondary economy (clothing, running shoes, cars, TVs, medical equipment, household appliances, computers and electronic equipment, the steel industry).
- In response, US capitalists maintained growth and profits through computers, automation, the export of industries and jobs to Asia and Latin America, and the introduction of lower-paid women and immigrants into the labor force. Finally, capitalism had no labor shortage. This led to the weakening of the bargaining power of the labor movement and the flattening of wages, while productivity and profits continued to increase.
- The workers' reaction to this loss of wage was to work longer and harder. But that wasn't enough. The rest of the family—women, the retired, and teenagers—entered the workforce, tying to survive and maintain their newly acquired "middle class" status.
- To further offset the effect of falling wages (while production and profits soared), there was a great expansion of debt, for excessive borrowing was the only way left to maintain the living standards of the population at the time when wealth was going to the elite. First, there was borrowing against

the house and then credit cards with steadily rising interest rates.
- The working class was robbed twice: (1) the surplus their labor produced and (2) the interest on the loans lent back to them in order to buy commodities.
- This crisis had a different consequence for the capitalist class. With the weakening of labor and ensuing loss of wage increases and increase in worker productivity through technology and reduction of the workforce through outsourcing, capitalists' profits kept rising. Rising profits allowed capitalists to increase CEO and manager salaries, increase mergers and acquisitions of corporations, increase lobbying for reducing corporate taxes to the point where the *New York Times* reported in 2008 that most major corporations paid no taxes, and allow more immigration to lower workers' wages.
- America's tax base was diminished due to the loss of the manufacturing base by runaway-tax-dodging multinational corporations. The business elites blamed the problem on big government and high taxes, which turned into the political conservatives' mantra, which led to the cutting of government services, hurting the working class.
- Because of the premise that capitalism must grow and create profits, the banks and other financial businesses found new innovative ways to use their money other than investment in production. They moved to increase wealth in the financial sector—the tertiary economy.

Tertiary Economy

There is another part of the economy that we can call the tertiary economy (often described as the financial economy). Here is where capitalists set up an arrangement to provide the money they need to keep production growing. It is composed of banks, advertisers, insurance companies, security exchanges, pension funds, legal firms, and investment institutions, and is designed to lubricate the wheel of capitalism (the secondary economy).

- For the past thirty years, capitalist industrial production declined from 25 to 13 percent of the gross domestic product, while at the same time, financial services expanded from 11 to 21 percent.[7] Although the tertiary economy has grown, the secondary economy, dealing with production, is still the major force. The United States is still the world's major manufacturing economy,[8] although China is about to overtake us.
- More and more capitalists preferred to speculate on financial and property markets rather than invest in new industrial enterprises, secure raw materials and machines, and train new staff. Even established secondary economy industries like General Motors, Ford, and General Electric started relying on their financial divisions for more of their profits—they turned themselves into banks to finance their products.
- As profitability declined in productive sectors, the monetary authorities tried to boost growth by lowering interest rates, printing more money, or making contracts for bonds, mortgages, and other financial instruments. Money capital grew, giving the appearance that there was plenty to reinvest.
- But that was an illusion, since capital wasn't based on profits from the productive sector. New and complicated financial instruments were created to finance the buying of stocks, buildings, and houses. But this capital reached mind-boggling levels when the derivative markets (contracts to buy and sell bonds by a certain date) reached ten times the world's GDP. This discrepancy could not last. The trigger for the downfall was housing.
- One of the most effective profit makers was the mortgage industry, which could make profits on the dream that all

Americans can buy a house on credit. This was effective, because the houses historically gained in price.
- As their credit cards maxed out, consumers moved to taking out cash equity from their inflated house values. People relied on second and third mortgages and home equity loans.
- The capitalists saw how powerful the financial sector was in producing profits, and they convinced the government through their lobbyists to relax the regulations that were placed on the financial sector due to the catastrophe of the Great Depression of 1929. For example, the cancellation of the Glass-Steagall Act of 1933, which separated lending from investing, allowed banks to become investment corporations as well—also passing the Commodity Futures Modernization Act of 2000 that deregulated all over-the-counter derivatives, including the credit default swaps and many other instruments that were involved in the 2008 crisis.[9]
- The shift of capital from the secondary economy to the tertiary economy allowed the capitalists to make radically increased profits. In 2007, the US CEOs were paid 344 times the pay of workers. Now the top hedge and private-equity fund managers earned many thousand of times as much as the average US worker (who was still working).
- Excessive profits could be increased when new homebuyers were lured into predatory subprime and adjustable-rate mortgages with the assurance that housing prices would continue to rise. These loans were bundled up with good loans and sold to speculators who assumed housing prices would continue to rise. This led to a house of cards that banks around the world invested in.
- The contention among most analysts is that the spark for the crisis of 2008 was primarily due to a combination of bad real estate loans and poor regulation of financial derivatives. Since the working class had to finally face levels of debt

that were unsustainable, its consumption diminished, unemployment increased, and capitalism, which was based on expanding mass consumption, went into crisis.
- While the working class went into debt, losing income, benefits, jobs, and security, the wealthy speculated in the new financial instruments and, using their wealth and power, got the government to minimize regulations and oversight over the financial structure. They also used their financial support of both political parties and the weakness of the labor movement to make sure there could be no repetition of a New Deal program similar to the one FDR used in the previous depression. In addition, the ruling class pressured the government to respond to the crisis by helping bail out the perpetrators, the financial institutions: banks, large corporations, and the stock markets. Finally, the ruling class pushed for austerity programs: extreme cutbacks in government spending, especially on social programs and essential services.
- This is an overview of the part of the story that many books and films have revealed.[10] But most of these overviews failed to seriously examine another aspect of capitalism, the effects of the primary economy on the crisis.

Primary Economy

The primary economy of nature makes the secondary economy possible. It includes sunlight and energy resources derived from ancient sunlight like coal and oil, the biological cycles, soil fertility, pollination, hydrological cycles, and the tectonic process that gives us access to metals and minerals. Without nature, no human economy would exist. This seems more obvious as we enter the era of peak oil, ecocatastrophe, species decline, ecological destruction, and the number-one issue for humanity, climate change. Before this moment, very few economists recognized the fundamental importance of nature. (A group that did early on included James Maitland [Earl of Lauderdale], Karl Marx, Henry George, Thorstein Veblen, and Frederick Soddy).[11] Today, though, in a time of pending environmental destruction, climate change, and peak oil, such unorthodox views are making a comeback, even though most mainstream economists either ignore the impact of nature or assume that nature is an inexhaustible resource.[12]

- By paying close attention to the relationship between the primary and secondary economy, we see that carbon-based (oil, coal, gas) energy is needed to keep factories running, power the cities, and produce the crops that feed humanity.
- But we are beginning to recognize that our energy source is finite. Petroleum becomes harder to locate and more expensive to extract. More capital is needed for oil shale extraction and deep-ocean drilling, as well as financing a military that will maintain access to "our" petroleum resources throughout the world.
- More oil is needed by other growing economies (China, India). Thus, US capitalism's need to grow becomes more challenging and more costly, ultimately requiring military bullying or wars to control oil and other resources.[13]
- Workers are the first to feel the effects of the increase in oil prices through losing their jobs or having their workweeks reduced as corporations begin to react to the energy shortage. Also, getting to and from work costs more, as does the heating of homes and apartments, food, and consumer goods.
- In a campaign to help America grow prosperous, the capitalist class, holding on to its growth perspective, directs its media and political agents to obscure the connection between fossil fuels and environmental destruction, support the extension of oil pipelines, drill for new oil, increase shale extraction, continue mountaintop coal removal, attack

regulations, weaken government agencies designed to protect the environment, and ignore alternative energy sources like sun, wind, and tidal.
- The capitalist class also uses its media and political power to cover up or destroy its enemies: labor unions, environmentalists, advocates of increased regulations, and the Occupy Wall Street movement.
- In the preceding story of the crisis, Wolff pointed out that the beginning of the working class's decline in wages occurred at about the time that the Arab oil boycott forced the world's politicians to recognize the importance of controlling fossil fuels for the maintenance and continuance of the secondary economy.
- Paying attention to the primary economy and analyzing its effect on the secondary and tertiary economies leads to the conclusion that economic health is as dependant on oil prices as the financial sector and housing market, and fluctuations in the world oil prices are a significant factor in analyzing the crisis in 2008. A few thinkers have attempted such a task,[14] but they are in a minority. Their proposals are ignored or not taken seriously by the proponents of the growth and profit.
- Jeff Rubin, chief economist at CIBC World Markets, pointed out that the three longest US recessions since the Great Depression coincided with high oil prices. The first followed the 1973 embargo (started in November 1973) and the second in July 1981. The latest began in December 2007 and lasted eighteen months.[15]
- Rubin concluded that the often-blamed mortgage default was a symptom of the high oil prices. As evidence, he points to the fact high oil prices caused Japan and Europe to enter a recession before the 2008 catastrophe hit the United States.[16]
- Following the work of Dr. Nouriel Roubini,[17] who argued

that high oil prices caused the recent financial crisis, Professor James D. Hamilton, in his paper on historical oil shocks,[18] demonstrated that economic downturns followed each of the major postwar oil shocks after World War II (the Suez Crisis of 1956–57, the OPEC oil embargo of 1973–1974, the Iranian Revolution of 1978–1979, the Iran-Iraq War in 1980, the first Persian Gulf War in 1990–91, and the oil price spike of 2007–2008).

- According to economist Eric Zencey, "An infinite growth economy runs into the limits of a finite world. The financial crisis is the environmental crisis... we can't solve the former until we start solving the latter."[19]
- As fossil fuels are more difficult to extract and as more capital is required to accomplish this task, capitalists will look for better places and methods to find profit, turning to the tertiary economy or to ways to diminish the cost of worker pay: outsourcing, mechanization, and so on.
- The critique of capitalism will probably not be acknowledged or accepted unless there is pressure from below. That is the task of the combined working class social justice and environmental movement.
- In the meantime, as productivity falls and the secondary economy declines, we can see that the profit drive of capitalism will begin to take advantage of the breakdown by cannibalizing its own infrastructure by profiting on economic crises, using Naomi Klein's shock doctrine. Unless it organizes with the environmentalists and fights back, the working class will be decimated by layoffs, destruction of unions, and loss of pension funds. Education and social programs will disappear and become privatized for the rich under a new brand of American austerity, described earlier as catabolic capitalism.

GLOSSARY

The meanings in this glossary often depend on the perspective of the group that is doing the defining. Whenever applicable, I indicate which perspective is applied: the capitalist class or the working class. No designation means the definition is acceptable to both perspectives.

Accumulation of capital (working class) is the central dynamic of capitalist society. It is the repeated and progressive conversion of surplus value into fresh capital.

Adultism describes behaviors and attitudes based on the assumption that adults are better than youth and thus entitled to act upon them without their agreement. Social institutions, laws, customs, and attitudes reinforce this mistreatment.

Ageism is any attitude, action, or institutional structure that subordinates or mistreats a person or group because of age. Social institutions, laws, customs, and attitudes reinforce this mistreatment.

Alienation is a certain loss of self, accompanied by feelings of unhappiness or psychological discontent, arising from conditions of human bondage.

Alienation (working class—applying economic concreteness to the above definition) occurs when workers in capitalist society do not produce freely as an expression of their true human potential and aspirations but under coercive conditions that dictate what and how they must produce.

There are four aspects of alienation:
1. Alienation from the product of labor: the product of labor becomes an alien object that workers do not control and that comes to rule over them.
2. Alienation from process of labor: in the process of labor, humans must suppress their unique human qualities as potentially free producers and subordinate themselves to external control; labor becomes merely a means to an end rather than a means of self-development.
3. Alienation from other workers: workers relate to others not as full human beings but as means to an end and as competitors for their jobs.
4. Alienation from human potential: workers suppress their unique human capacities for self-expression through creative labor (i.e., they suppress what distinguishes them as a species from other animals).

Bourgeoisie (working class) is that class of modern capitalists, owners of the means of production and employers of wage labor, who buy labor power to allow the expanded reproduction of capital.

Bourgeois society (working class) is the social formation where the commodity relation—the relation of buying and selling—has spread into every corner of life. Capitalist society.

Capital (working class) is an accumulation of money and cannot make its appearance in history until the circulation of commodities has given rise to the money relation. Secondly, the distinction between money as capital and money as currency arises from the difference in their form of circulation. Money that is acquired in order to buy something is just money, facilitating the exchange of commodities. On the other hand, capital is money that is used to buy something in order to sell it again. This means that capital exists only within the process of buying and selling, as money advanced only in order to get it back again.

Capital (capitalist class) is the final goods produced for use in the production of other goods (e.g., equipment, structures, or funds that finance the operation of a business).

Capitalism (working class) is the socioeconomic system where social relations are based on commodities for exchange, private ownership of the means of production, and the exploitation of wage labor, where market forces make basic distribution decisions. Also known as the secondary economy.

Capitalism (capitalist class) is an economic system where the means of production and distribution are privately or corporately owned, and development is proportionate to the accumulation and reinvestment of profits gained in a free market.

Capitalist class (working class) is composed of the owners of the means of production (the factories, corporations, material, etc.).

Catabolic capitalism (working class) is the point where capitalism is in crisis and doesn't have access to cheap energy necessary for maintaining growth, so it is forced to eat itself in order to maintain profits. For example, it confiscates and sells the stranded assets of the bankrupt industries and preys on people's desperation in their search for employment.

Class (working class) is that grouping of individuals with a common position in the production process, in relation to another group. An individual is a member of a class not because he or she makes a lot of money or goes to a high-status school but due to the place he or she occupies in society in relation to the ownership of the tools and raw materials needed to create commodities.

Class is an indicator of status. It is composed of individuals and families who are ranked similarly on several measurable criteria (wealth, education, neighborhood, etc.).

Class analysis (working class) is a method of analysis that is based on the recognition of the class nature of a society that is in constant flux, is organically related, and is historically developed.

Class society (working class) is a society composed of different social classes, first coming into place after the agricultural revolution.

Class struggle is the attempt to overcome a conflict when a social surplus of production exists, which makes it possible for one class to benefit by the exploitation of another.

Classless society would be lacking social or economic distinctions of class (e.g., band, tribal society, or communist society).

Classism (capitalist class) is the systematic oppression of the poor and those who work for wages by those who have access to control of the necessary resources. Social institutions, laws, customs, and attitudes reinforce this mistreatment. Note: this is not a working-class concept, because it focuses on effect rather than the cause.

Commodity (working class) is a product of labor that satisfies some human wants and is produced for sale on the market. The dominant feature of capitalist society is the production of goods as commodities.

Commodity (capitalist class) is an article of commerce or a product that can be used for commerce. In a narrow sense, products traded on an authorized commodity exchange. The types of commodities include agricultural products, metals, petroleum, foreign currencies, and financial instruments and index, to name a few.

Communism is an economic and political system based on the principle "From each according to their ability, to each according to their need." It stresses that the control of the means of producing economic goods in a society should reside in the hands of those who invest their labor for production. In its ideal form, social classes cease to exist, there are no coercive governmental structures, and everyone lives in abundance without supervision from a ruling class.

Coordinators are often known as the in-between group or the "middle class." Coordinators are workers; they are paid for their work; they are members of the working class. The coordinators work for salaries or wages, and their objective is to control, manage, and support the rest of the working class in order to efficiently continue the extraction of surplus value by the capitalist class. In spite of their position and nearness to the capitalist class and its values, they work for wages or salaries just as the working class does but often don't think of themselves in this way.

Division of labor (working class) is a system where different tasks are apportioned to different groups in a given society

Economics (working class) is the relation between classes in the process of production, exchange, distribution, and consumption of material wealth.

Economics (capitalist class) is the study of how best to allocate scarce resources among competing uses.

Exchange value and *use value* (working class) are the usefulness of a commodity versus the exchange equivalent by which the commodity is compared to other objects on the market. Use value is inextricably tied to the material uses where the object can actually be put, the human needs it fulfills. In the exchange of goods on the capitalist market, however, exchange value dominates: two commodities can be exchanged on the open market, because they are being compared to a third term that functions as their equivalent, a function that is eventually taken over by money. Exchange value must be distinguished from use value, because the exchange relation of commodities is characterized precisely by its abstraction from its use values. In capitalism, money takes the form of that equivalence; however, money in fact hides the real equivalent behind the exchange: labor. The more labor it takes to produce a product, the greater its value. As exchange values, all commodities are merely definite quantities of accrued labor time.

Exploitation (working class) is the making use of some vulnerability in another person in order to use him or her to attain one's own ends at that person's expense. In particular, wage labor is a form of exploitation where the working class is exploited by the capitalist class. The rate of exploitation is the proportion of unpaid surplus labor workers perform for their employers contrasted to the necessary labor workers perform, producing the value equivalent of the wages they are paid.

Feudalism was a political and economic structure of Europe from the ninth to about the fifteenth century. It is generally associated with predominantly small-scale agricultural production based on traditional patterns of land ownership and territory where the rights and duties of every member of society are defined by traditional inheritance and kinship relations.

Feudal society differs from band/tribal society in being a class society in which quite different and unequal rights and duties are enjoyed by different families, according to land rights, wealth, and social status inherited from previous generations.

Feudal society differs from slave society in that every class in feudal society has rights and is regarded as human, however lowly, whereas slaves have no rights at all and are treated as property rather than people.

Feudal society differs from bourgeois society, because bourgeois society operates outside the constraints imposed by traditional rights and ethics, being governed only by what can make a profit, in the market.

Financialization (otherwise know as the tertiary economy) is the financial economy whose job is to grease the wheels of the primary and secondary economies—to manage money in order to maximize return on invested capital. It is composed of banks, insurance companies, mortgage companies, advertisers, legal institutions, and investment institutions.

Fordism was named after Henry Ford (1863–1947), who developed a method of industrial management based on assembly-line methods, production of cheap, uniform commodities in high volume, and winning employee loyalty with good wages but was intolerant of unionism or employee participation.

Gini index measures the income inequality among the entire population of a country. The higher the number, the more income is being taken by a small group. If the income distribution is more equal, then the Gini index will be lower. The Gini index for the United States has risen since 1967. Some examples of Gini are the following: United States (in 2007) 45, Germany (in 2006) 27, Russia (in 2009) 42.2, Columbia (in 2009) 58.5, Sweden (in 2005) 23.

Globalization is an increasingly integrated global economy marked especially by free trade, free flow of capital, and the tapping of cheaper foreign labor markets.

Identity politics is that political space where various social groups struggle for recognition in bourgeois society (blacks, women, gays, youth, ecologists, and so on). These groups have their origin in the individualistic reaction to what was perceived as the ineffectiveness of collective struggles against state and institutional forms of oppression though class analysis.

Individualism and *collectivism*. Individualism is the practice that emphasizes the autonomy of the individual as against the community or social group. The word was first used in a translation of Tocqueville's *Democracy in America* in 1835.

Collectivism is the practice that emphasizes the priority of the community as a whole or the group as against the individual, originally as a synonym for common ownership of the means of production.

Individual (capitalist class) is a single person, animal, or thing of any kind; a thing or being incapable of separation or division without losing its identity, especially, a human being; a person. Capitalist society emphasizes the individual and promotes the ethics of autonomy.

Individual (working class) is a social being whose essence is the aggregate of social relations.

Labor (working class) is productive work, especially physical work done for wages. In ancient times, slaves did much of the work. In the feudal period, agricultural labor was mainly performed by the serf. In medieval towns, however, the skilled artisans of the craft guilds became influential citizens. Many manual labor jobs were eliminated with the introduction of machinery (mideighteenth century), thus creating a labor surplus. With increased competition for jobs and consequent decreasing wages, a form of labor contract came into use in Great Britain and its colonies, called indenture, where individuals could hire themselves out for a certain number of years, either for a lump sum of money or to pay off a debt. This practice disappeared by the end of the nineteenth century. From the last quarter of the nineteenth century, the condition of most manual labor has improved slowly in industrial countries through organization, permitting collective bargaining with employers and successful pressure on governments for protective legislation. The term "labor" is today most frequently used to signify organized labor.

Labor (capitalist class) is a factor of production; the skills and abilities to produce goods and services.

Labor power (working class) is the combination of those mental and physical capabilities existing in a human being, which he or she exercises whenever he or she produces a use value of any description. Labor power is a commodity.

Market is a mechanism that allows people to trade, normally governed by the theory of supply and demand. Markets work by placing many interested sellers in one place, thus making them easier to find for prospective buyers. A market economy relies primarily on interactions between buyers and sellers to distribute resources, in contrast either to a command economy or to a nonmarket economy.

Means of production (working class) is the land, natural resources, and technology that are necessary for the production of material goods.

Mental labor and *manual labor* (working class) are two interconnected modes of human activity. Mental and manual labor were an undivided whole in band/tribal society. Mental and manual labor were possible only on the basis of the division of labor. With the emergence of private property, classes, and the state, mental labor became the privilege of the ruling capitalist class and their coordinators. In ancient times, the status of manual laborers was low, as slaves did most of the physical labor. This continued into the feudal period, where skilled laborers were seen as artisans and could aspire to become influential citizens.

Middle class (working class) or sometimes "the middle classes," is a very general term indicating all those classes that lie in between the ruling capitalist class and the producing class. See *coordinators*.

Mode of production (working class) is the type of economy a society has. It is the combination of the means of production and the social relationships people enter into as they acquire and use the means of production. It is, within any given society, the mode of production changes in any one of the different epochs of history—for example, agricultural society, industrial society, hunting and gathering, or currently, the capitalist mode of production.

Neoliberalism argues that the control of the economy must shift from the public sector to the private sector. Governments must reduce deficit spending, limit subsidies, reform tax law and broaden the tax base, open up markets to trade by limiting protectionism, privatize state-run businesses, and back deregulation.

Oppression is a kind of injustice; the inequitable use of authority, law, or physical force to prevent others from being free or equal.

Patriarchy is social organization marked by the male domination of ownership and control at all levels in society that maintains and operates the system of gender discrimination. This structure of control is justified in terms of patriarchal ideology: ideas based on a belief in male superiority and sometimes the claim that the gender division of labor is based on biology or even based on scripture.

Patriotism is love for or devotion to one's country.

Patriotism (working class) "assumes that our globe is divided into little spots, each one surrounded by an iron gate. Those who had the fortune of being born on some particular spot, consider themselves better, nobler, grander, and more intelligent than the living beings inhabiting any other spot. It is, therefore, the duty of everyone living on that chosen spot to fight, kill, and die in the attempt to impose his superiority upon all others" (Emma Goldman).

Patriotism, along with nationalism is one of the time-honored tools for dividing workers into artificially antagonistic camps, both internationally and domestically. Foreign workers are portrayed as enemies/competitors, while minorities within the domestic working class are singled out as enemies of the state. This has become evident since September 11, 2001, as Muslims and Arabs have been designated as the enemy "race" at home and abroad. Conceit, arrogance, and egotism are the essentials of patriotism.

Peak oil designates the problem of the peak in global oil production. Oil is a finite, nonrenewable resource that has powered economic and population growth over the last century and a half. The rate of oil production has grown almost every year of the last century. After we use half of the original reserves, oil production stops growing and begins to decline, to "peak." This means the end of cheap oil and the potential of severe economic and social consequences. Various predictions of peak oil vary, but most experts believe it will happen between 2005 and 2020.

Petty bourgeoisie (working class) are the members of the lower-middle social classes. They were seen as servants of the bourgeois class who in turn were seen as servants of the aristocracy. Now described as small-business owners.

Political economy was developed in eighteenth century as the study of the economies of states (polities), in contrast to the theory of the physiocrats, in which land was seen as the source of all wealth. Political economy proposed the labor theory of value, where labor is the real source of value.
In the late nineteenth century, the term "political economy" was replaced by the term "economics," which placed the study of its economy on a mathematical basis rather than studying the structural relationships within production and consumption.

Precariat are workers whose lives are difficult because they have little or no job security and few employment rights. As a result of the massive deindustrialization and public policies springing out of neoliberalism, the labor force has found its status to be temporary or temporarily nonexistent.

Primary economy is the finite aspect of capitalism that the earth provides and humans transform: fish, forests, animals, the biological cycles, soil fertility, pollination, hydrological cycles, the tectonic process that gives us access to metals, minerals, and fossil fuels.

Private property (working class) is any property that is owned by one individual or a small group of individuals and used to make a profit.

Private property (capitalist class) is a fundamental economic institution where resources (property) are owned and controlled by households and businesses (the private sector) rather than government (the public sector). Private property provides critical incentives for the efficient operation of competitive market and a market-oriented economy. Under private property ownership, control over resources is relinquished (that is sold) when the owners are compensated for their opportunity costs.

Production and *consumption* (working class) are two inseparable aspects of the production and reproduction of human life, but in modern society, these concepts have become separated.

Production and *consumption* (capitalist class). Production is manufacturing, mining, or growing something (usually in large quantities) for sale. Consumption is expenditure by consumers on final goods and services.

Profit (working class) is the unpaid labor expropriated from workers by a capitalist and distributed by various means among the capitalist class, measured in proportion to the total capital invested. See *surplus value*.

Profit (capitalist class) is the difference between total revenue and total cost.

Proletariat is that class in society that lives entirely from the sale of its labor power and does not draw profit from any kind of capital, whose sole existence depends on the demand for labor. See *working class*.

Racism is the belief that some races are inherently superior (physically, intellectually, or culturally) to others and therefore have a right to dominate them. In the United States, racism, particularly by whites against blacks, has created racial tension and conflict in virtually all aspects of American society.

Ruling capitalist class (working class) is that portion of the capitalist class that controls the dominant political and cultural institutions in society. The ruling capitalist class is not necessarily unified on all issues.

Sexism is prejudice or discrimination based on gender. Like the other "isms," sexism can be both personal and institutional (see *patriarchy*).

Slave society (working class) is a society where the fundamental class conflict is based on the division of society into masters and slaves, with slaves being the dominant producing class that is controlled by masters.

Slave society (capitalist class) is a society based on the control of a person against his or her will, enforced by violence or other clear forms of coercion. It generally occurs for the purpose of securing the labor from the person concerned.

Socialism is the theory of the ownership and operation of the means of production and distribution by society rather than by private individuals, with all members of the community sharing in the work and the products. Socialism is the transition phase between capitalism and communism, defined as "abolition of private property."

Status is the mainstream understanding of class. Styles of life led by individuals that indicate their standing in the community. Seen as a matter of culture and identity, a position relative to that of others.

Surplus labor (working class) is the unpaid labor a worker performs for his or her employer; labor performed in the creation of surplus value.

Surplus value (working class) is unpaid labor that is the source of profit for the capitalist. The difference between the price of a product produced by labor and the value of labor itself in terms of the wages paid to workers.

Taylorism was named after Frederick Winslow Taylor (1856–1915), the American inventor and engineer who was the first to make a scientific study of industrial management. Taylor's management corresponds to the early development of mass production and assembly-line manufacture and is characterized by extreme elaboration of the division of labor, the reduction of work to machine-like, repetitive operations, and extreme labor discipline and supervision of work aimed at minimizing production time per unit of commodity.

Tribal society is a description that covers a vast array of societies, from the earliest humans who first stood upright and who have long since disappeared from the earth, up to the citizens of the early Greek polis before about 600 BC, and indigenous people in many remote parts of the world today, who maintain herds, live in settled villages, and engage in a certain amount of trade. What characterizes tribal society is that there are no social classes. (Anthropologists categorize societies by social complexity, from bands and tribes to chiefdoms and states. Currently, about 250,000 people live in band-level societies, who subsist mainly from gathering wild plants and hunting.)

Wage labor is the mode of production in which the laborer sells his or her capacity to work as a commodity.

Wage slavery (working class) is the condition where a person must sell his or her labor power, submitting to the authority of an employer, in order to survive. Workers ironically refer to it as the condition where you are free to starve.

Working class is that class in society that lives entirely from the sale of its labor power and does not draw profit from any kind of capital.

BIBLIOGRAPHY

Albert, Michael. *Parecon: Life After Capitalism.* New York: Verso Books, 2003.

Amin, Samir. *Revolutionary Objectives in the Twenty-First Century.* New York: Monthly Review, 2001.

Angell, Marcia. *The Truth About the Drug Companies: How They Deceive Us and What To Do About It.* New York: Random House, 2004.

Alperovitz, Gar. *What Then Must We Do?: Straight Talk About the Next American Revolution.* Vermont: Chelsea Green, 2013.

Arnold, Al. *Moving Mountains and Molehills: Local Politics 101.* BookSurge.com, 2005.

Aronowitz, Stanley. *How Class Works.* New Haven, CT: Yale University Press, 2003.

———. *The Knowledge Factory: Dismantling the Corporate University and Creating True Higher Learning.* Boston: Beacon Press, 2000.

Bakan, Joel. *The Corporation: The Pathological Pursuit of Profit and Power.* New York: Free Press, 2005.

Barbour, Ian, Harvey Brooks, Sanford Lakoff, and John Opie. *Energy and American Values*. New York: Praeger, 1982.

Bardacke, Frank. *Trampling Out the Vintage: Cesar Chavez and the Two Souls of the United Farm Workers*. New York: Verso Books, 2011.

Bardhan, Ashok Deo, and Cynthia A. Kroll. "The New Wave of Outsourcing." *Research Report Fisher Center for Real Estate and Urban Economics*. Berkeley, CA: University of California, 2003.

Bari, Judi. *Timber Wars*. Monroe, ME: Common Courage Press, 1994.

Barlett, Donald L.. and James B. Steele. *The Betrayal of the American Dream*. New York: Public Affairs, 2012.

Baudrillard, Jean. *America*. New York: Verso Books, 1993.

Beard, Charles A. *An Economic Interpretation of the Constitution of the United States*. New York: Free Press, 1986.

Bell, Daniel. *The Coming of Post-Industrial Society*. New York: Basic Books, 1973.

Bernays, Edward. *Propaganda*. New York: Ig Publishing, 2005.

Bircham, Emma (Editor). Hsiao, Andrew (Editor), Charlton, John (Editor) *Anti-Capitalism: A Field Guide to the Global Justice Movement*. New York: W. W. Norton, 2004.

Blackburn, Robin. *The Making of New World Slavery: From the Baroque to the Modern, 1492–1800*. New York: Verso Books, 1998.

Blackmon, Douglas A. *Slavery by Another Name: The Re-Enslavement of Black Americans From the Civil War to World War II*. New York: Anchor Books, 2008.

Bluestone, Barry. *The Polarization of American Society: Victims, Suspects, and Mysteries to Unravel.* New York: Twentieth Century Fund Press, 1995.

Bowles, Samuel, and Herbert Gintess. *Schooling in Capitalist America.* New York: Basic Books, 1976.

Brenner, Aaron, Robert Brenner, and Cal Winslow. *Rebel Rank and File: Labor Militancy and Revolt from Below During the Long 1970s.* New York: Verso Books, 2010.

Broswimmer, Franz J. *Ecocide: A Short History of the Mass Extinction of Species.* London: Pluto Press, 2002.

Burns, Joe. *Reviving the Strike: How Working People Can Regain Power and Transform America.* New York: Ig Publishing, 2011.

Castells, Manuel. *The Information Age.* Vol. 3. Cambridge, MA: Blackwell, 1998.

Chomsky, Noam. *Necessary Illusions: Thought Control in Democratic Societies.* Boston: South End Press, 1989.

Chomsky, Noam, and Edward S. Herman. *Manufacturing Consent.* New York: Pantheon Books, 1988.

Cleaver, Harry. *Reading Capital Politically.* Oakland, CA: AK Press, 2000.

Clements, Jeffrey. *Corporations Are Not People: Why They Have More Rights Than You Do and What You Can Do about It.* San Francisco: Berrett-Koehler, 2011.

Cohen, Jean L. *Class and Civil Society.* Amherst, MA: University of Massachusetts Press, 1982.

Collins, Craig. *Toxic Loopholes: Failures and Future Prospects for Environmental Law.* New York: Cambridge University Press, 2010.

_____. *Marx and Mother Nature*. Unpublished manuscript, 1982.

Commoner, Barry. *The Closing Circle: Nature, Man, and Technology*. New York: Bantam Books, 1974.

_____. *The Poverty of Power*. New York: Bantam Books, 1976.

_____. *The Politics of Energy*. New York: Knopf. 1979.

_____. *Making Peace with the Planet*. New York: Pantheon Books, 1990.

Conner, Cliff. *A People's History of Science: Miners, Midwives, and "Low Mechanicks."* New York: Nation Books, 2005.

Cookson, Peter W., and Caroline Hodges Persell. *Preparing for Power: America's Elite Boarding Schools*. New York: Basic Books, 1987.

Countryman, Edward. *Americans: A Collision of Histories*. New York: Hill and Wang, 1996.

Cowie, Jefferson. *Stayin' Alive: The 1970s and the Last Days of the Working Class* New York: New Press 2010.

Croteau, David. *Politics and the Class Divide*. Philadelphia: Temple University Press, 1995.

Dalphin, John. *The Persistence of Social Inequality in America*. Cambridge, MA: Schenkman Books, 1987.

Davis, Mike. *Prisoners of the American Dream*. New York: Verso Books, 1999.

_____. *Planet of Slums*. New York: Verso Books, 2006.

Daly, Herman E. and Joshua Farley. *Ecological Economics, Second Edition: Principles and Applications*. Washington, DC: Island Press, 2011.

Dalphin, John. *The Persistence of Social Inequality in America.* Cambridge, MA : Schenkman Books, 1987.

De Graaf, John, ed. *Take Back Your Time.* San Francisco: Berrett-Koehler, 2003.

Diamond, Jared. *Guns, Germs, and Steel.* New York: Norton Paperbacks, 1999.

Dowd, Douglas. *Capitalism and Its Economics: A Critical History.* Ann Arbor, MI: Pluto Press, 2004.

Drew, Elizabeth. *The Corruption of American Politics: What Went Wrong and Why.* New York: Overlook Press, 1999.

Domhoff, G. William. *Who Rules America?* New York: McGraw-Hill, 2001.

_____. *Bohemian Grove and Other Retreats: A Study in Ruling-Class Cohesiveness.* New York: Harper Books, 1974.

Dublin, Thomas. *Women at Work: The Transformation of Work and Community in Lowell, Massachusetts, 1826–1860.* New York: Columbia University, 1993.

Du Boff, Richard. *Accumulation and Power: An Economic History of the United States.* Armonk, NY: M. E. Sharpe, 1989.

Dye, Thomas R. *Who's Running America?: The Reagan Years.* Englewood Cliffs, NJ: Prentice-Hall, 1983.

Dyer-Witheford, Nick. *Cyber-Marx.* Chicago: University of Illinois Press, 1999.

Edwards, David. *Burning All Illusions.* Boston: South End Press, 1996.

_____. *The Compassionate Revolution: Radical Politics and Buddhism.* Devon, UK: Green Books, 1998.

Ehrenberg, Margaret. *Women in Prehistory.* London: British Museum Publications, 1989.

Ehrenreich, Barbara. *Fear of Falling.* New York: Harper Perennial, 1990.

_____. *Nickel and Dimed: On (Not) Getting by in America.* New York: Henry Holt, 2001.

Ellison, Sharon. *Taking the War Out of Our Words.* Berkeley, CA: Bay Tree Press, 2002.

Engels, Frederick. *Dialectics of Nature.* London: Lawrence & Wishart, 1940.

Enzensberger, Hans Magnus. *The Consciousness Industry.* New York: Seabury Press, 1974.

Faux, Jeff. *The Global Class War.* Hoboken, NJ: John Wiley & Sons, 2006.

Federici, Silvia. *Caliban and the Witch: Women, the Body, and Primitive Accumulation.* New York: Automedia, 2004.

Feinstein, Andrew. *The Shadow World: Inside the Global Arms Trade.* New York: Picador Press 2012.

Fitch, Robert. *Solidarity for Sale: How Corruption Destroyed the Labor Movement and Undermined America's Promise.* New York: Public Affairs Press, 2006.

Fitzgerald, Frances. *America Revised: History Schoolbooks in the Twentieth Century.* Boston: Little, Brown, 1979.

Freeman, Richard B., and Joel Rogers. *What Workers Want*. Ithaca, NY: Cornell University Press, 1999.

Freire, Paolo. *Pedagogy of the Oppressed*. New York: Continuum, 1993.

Gonzalez, Juan. *Fallout: The Environmental Consequences of the World Trade Center Collapse*. New York: New Press, 2004.

Gould, Stephen Jay. *Leonardo's Mountain of Clams and the Diet of Worms*. New York: Harmony Books, 1998.

Gray, Virginia, and Russell Hanson. *Politics in the American States: A Comparative Analysis*. Washington, DC: CQ Press, 2007.

Greer, John Michael. *The Long Descent*. Gabriola Island, BC: New Society, 2008.

_____. *The Wealth of Nature: Economics as if Survival Mattered*. Gabriola Island, BC: New Society, 2011.

Griffin, Donald R. *Animal Minds: Beyond Cognition to Consciousness*. Chicago: University of Chicago Press, 2001.

Haenfler, Ross. Johnson, Brett. Klocke, Brian. Jones, Ellis. *The Better World Handbook: From Good Intentions to Everyday Actions* Boulder, CO: New Society, 2001.

Hansen, Valerie. *The Silk Road: A New History*. New York: Oxford University Press, 2012.

Harman, Chris. *A People's History of the World*. London, UK: Bookmarks, 1999.

Harrington, Michael. *The Other America*. New York: Touchstone Books, 1962.

Harris, Marvin. *Cannibals and Kings*. New York: Viking, 1991.

Hawken, Paul. *Blessed Unrest: How the Largest Social Movement in History is Restoring Grace, Justice, and Beauty to the World.* New York: Penguin Press, 2008.

Hayes, Christopher. *Twilight of the Elites: America after Meritocracy.* New York: Crown, 2012.

Heilbroner, Robert L. and Lester Thurow. *Economics Explained.* New York: Simon & Schuster, 1994.

Heinberg, Richard. *The Party's Over: Oil, War, and the Fate of Industrial Societies.* Gabriola Island, BC: New Society, 2005.

_____. *The End of Growth: Adapting to Our New Economic Reality.* Gabriola Island, BC: New Society, 2011.

_____. *Peak Everything: Waking up to the Century of Declines.* Gabriola Island, BC: New Society, 2007.

Hilton, Rodney J. *The Transition from Feudalism to Capitalism.* London: Macmillan, 1985.

Hochschild, Arlie Russell. *The Managed Heart: Commercialization of Human Feeling.* Berkeley: U. C. Press, 1983.

Hochschild, Arlie Russell and Barbara Ehrenreich, ed. *Global Woman: Nannies, Maids, and Sex Workers in the New Economy.* New York: Henry Holt, 2002.

Holmgren, David. *Future Scenarios: How Communities Can Adapt to Peak Oil and Climate Change.* White River Junction, VT: Chelsea Green, 2009.

Homer, Richmond Lattimore, trans. *The Iliad.* Chicago: University of Chicago Press, 1961.

hooks, bell. *Teaching to Transgress.* New York: Routledge, 1994.

Humphries, Jane. *Childhood and Child Labour in the British Industrial Revolution.* New York: Cambridge University Press, 2011.

Janssen, Marco A. *Working Together: Collective Action, the Commons, and Multiple Methods in Practice.* Princeton, NJ: Princeton University Press, 2010.

Johnson, Chalmers. *Nemesis.* New York: Henry Holt, 2006.

Johnston, David Cay. *The Fine Print: How Big Companies Use Plain English to Rob You Blind.* New York: Penguin Books, 2012.

———. *Free Lunch.* New York: Penguin, 2007.

Katz, Michael. *The Undeserving Poor.* New York: Pantheon Books, 1990.

Kawachi, Ichiro, and Bruce P. Kennedy. *The Health of Nations: Why Inequality Is Harmful to Your Health.* New York: New Press, 2002.

Kelly, Charles M. *Class War in America.* Santa Barbara, CA: Fithian Press, 2000.

Kimmel, Michael. *The Gendered Society.* New York: Oxford University Press, 2000.

Kivel, Paul. *You Call This a Democracy?* New York: Apex Press, 2004.

Klein, Naomi. *The Shock Doctrine: The Rise of Disaster Capitalism.* New York: Henry Holt, 2008.

Kovel, Joel. *The Enemy of Nature.* London: Zed Books, 2002.

Kunstler, James Howard. *The Long Emergency: Surviving the Converging Catastrophes of the Twenty-First Century.* New York: Grove Atlantic, 2005.

Landau, Saul. *The Business of America: How Consumers Have Replaced Citizens and How We Can Reverse the Trend.* New York: Routledge Press, 2004.

Leacock, Eleanor. *Myths of Male Dominance.* New York: Monthly Review, 1981.

Leondar-Wright, Betsy. *Class Matters: Cross-Class Alliance Building for Middle-Class Activists.* Gabriola Island, BC: New Society, 2006.

Lerro, Bruce. *Power in Eden: The Emergence of Gender Hierarchies in the Ancient World.* Vancouver, BC: Trafford Press, 2005.

Lessig, Lawrence. *The Future of Ideas: The Fate of Commons in a Connected World.* New York: Vintage Books, 2001.

Lichtman, Richard. *The Production of Desire: The Integration of Psychoanalysis into Marxist Theory.* New York: Free Press, 1982.

Lilley, Sasha, David McNally, Eddie Yuen, and James Davis. *Catastrophism: The Apocalyptic Politics of Collapse and Rebirth.* Oakland, CA: PM Press, 2012.

Linkon, Sherry Lee, ed. *Teaching Working Class.* Amherst, MA: University of Massachusetts Press, 1999.

Lipsitz, George. *Class and Culture in Cold War America: A Rainbow at Midnight.* New York: Praeger, 1981.

Loewen, James W. *Lies My Teacher Told Me.* New York: Touchstone Press, 1995.

Logan, Robert K. *Understanding New Media: Extending Marshall McLuhan.* New York: Peter Lang, 2010.

Mander, Jerry. *The Capitalism Papers: Fatal Flaws of an Obsolete System.* Berkeley, CA: Counterpoint, 2012.

McAlevey, Jane, and Bob Ostertag. *Raising Expectations (and Raising Hell): My Decade Fighting for the Labor Movement.* New York: Verso Books, 2012.

McCarthey, Nolan, Poole, Keith T., Rosenthal, Howard. *Polarized America: The Dance of Ideology and Unequal Riches.* Cambridge, MA: MIT Press 2006.

McChesney, Robert. *Digital Disconnect: How Capitalism is Turning the Internet Against Democracy.* New York: The New Press, 2013.

Maass, Alan. *The Case for Socialism.* Chicago: Haymarket Books, 2005.

MacLeod, Greg. *From Mondragon to America: Experiments in Community Economic Development.* Nova Scotia: University of Cape Breton Press, 1998.

Mandel, Ernest. *Marxist Economic Theory.* Vol. 1. New York: Monthly Review, 1968.

_____. *An Introduction to Marxist Economic Theory.* New York: Pathfinder Press, 1973.

Marcuse, Herbert. *One-Dimensional Man.* Boston: Beacon Press, 1964.

Marmot, Michael. *Status Syndrome: How Our Position on the Social Gradient Affects Longevity and Health.* London: Bloomsbury, 2004.

Martin, Christopher R. *Framed!: Labor and the Corporate Media.* Ithaca, NY: Cornell University Press, 2004.

Marx, Karl. *Capital, Vols. 1–3.* New York: Random House, 1977.

Marx, Karl, and Frederick Engels. *The Collected Works of Karl Marx and Frederick Engels.* Vol. 16. New York: International, 1980.

McCarthy, Nolan, Keith T. Poole, and Howard Rosenthal. *Polarized America: The Dance of Ideology and Unequal Riches*. Cambridge, MA: MIT Press, 2006.

McKnight, John. *The Careless Society: Community and Its Counterfeits*. New York: Basic Books, 1995.

McMurtry, John. *The Cancer Stage of Capitalism*. London: Pluto Press, 1999.

McNally, David. *Global Slump: The Economics and Politics of Crisis and Resistance*. Oakland, CA: PM Press, 2010.

Macleod, Greg. *From Mondragon to America: Experiments in Community Economic Development*. Sydney, NS: University College of Cape Breton Press, 1997

Meadows, Donella H., Jorgen Randers, and Dennis L. Meadows. *Limits to Growth: The 30-Year Update*. White River Junction, VT: Chelsea Green, 2004.

Meltzer, Milton. *Slavery: A World History*. Cambridge, MA: Da Capo Press, 1993.

Merchant, Carolyn. *Radical Ecology: The Search for a Livable World*. New York: Routledge, 1992.

Meszaros, Istvan. *The Challenge and Burden of Historical Time: Socialism in the Twenty-First Century*. New York: Monthly Review, 2009.

Mielants, Eric. *The Origins of Capitalism and the "Rise of the West."* Philadelphia: Temple University Press, 2007.

Mies, Maria. *Patriarchy and Accumulation on a World Scale, Second Edition*. London: Zed Books, 1998.

Milanovic, Branco. *Worlds Apart: Measuring International and Global Inequality.* Princeton, NJ: Princeton University Press, 2005.

Moody, Kim. *An Injury to All.* New York: Verso Books, 1988.

Nace, Ted. *Gangs of America: The Rise of Corporate Power and the Disabling of Democracy.* San Francisco: Barrett-Koehler, 2003.

Neumann, Osha. *Up Against the Wall, Motherf**ker: A Memoir of the '60s, with Notes for Next Time.* New York: Seven Stories Press, 2008.

Nore, Petter, and Terisa Turner, eds. *Oil and Class Struggle.* London: Zed Books, 1980.

O'Brien, Mary. *Reproducing the World: Essays in Feminist Theory.* Boulder, CO: Westview Press, 1989.

Ollman, Bertell. *Alienation.* New York: Cambridge University Press, 1971.

———. *How to Take an Exam and Remake the World.* Montreal: Black Rose Books, 2001.

Ostrom, Elinor. *Governing the Commons: The Evolution of Institutions for Collective Action.* New York: Cambridge University Press, 1990.

Parenti, Christian. *Lockdown America: Police and Prisons in the Age of Crisis.* New York: Verso Books, 1999.

Parenti, Michael. *Inventing Reality: The Politics of News Media.* New York: Saint Martin's Press, 1993.

———. *History as Mystery.* San Francisco: City Lights Books, 1999.

———. *Democracy for the Few.* Belmont, CA: Wadsworth, 2001.

Perelman, Michael. *The Invention of Capitalism: Classical Political Economy and the Secret History of Primitive Accumulation*. Durham, NC: Duke University Press, 2000.

_____. *The Invisible Handcuffs of Capitalism: How Market Tyranny Stifles the Economy by Stunting Workers*. New York: Monthly Review, 2011.

Perkins, John. *Confessions of an Economic Hit Man*. New York: Penguin Books, 2004.

Perrow, Charles. *Organizing America: Wealth, Power, and the Origins of Corporate Capitalism*. Princeton, NJ: Princeton University Press, 2002.

Phillips, Kevin. *Bad Money*. New York: Viking, 2008.

Plato. *The Republic*. Indianapolis, IN: Hackett, 1992.

Polanyi, Karl. *The Great Transformation*. Boston: Beacon Press, 1957.

Pollin, Robert. *Back to Full Employment*. Boston: MIT Press, 2012.

Putnam, Robert D. *Bowling Alone: The Collapse and Revival of American Community*. New York: Simon & Schuster, 2000.

Quinn, Daniel. *Ishmael*. New York: Bantam Books, 1992.

Reiman, Jeffrey. *The Rich Get Richer and the Poor Get Prison: Ideology, Class and Criminal Justice*. New York: Allyn & Bacon, 2006.

Rich, Andrew. *Think Tanks, Public Policy, and the Politics of Expertise*. Cambridge: Cambridge University Press, 2004.

Rifkin, Jeremy, and Ted Howard. *Entropy: A New World View*. New York: Bantam Books, 1981.

Robbins, Alexandra. *Secrets of the Tomb: Skull and Bones, the Ivy League, and the Hidden Paths of Power.* New York: Little Brown, 2002.

Rodney, Walter. *How Europe Underdeveloped Africa.* Washington DC: Howard University Press, 1974.

Roediger, David. *The Wages of Whiteness: Race and the Making of the American Working Class.* New York: Verso Books, 1991.

Rose, Mike. *The Mind at Work: Valuing the Intelligence of the American Worker.* New York: Viking, 2004.

Rothernberg. Daniel. *With These Hands: The Hidden World of Migrant Farm Workers Today.* New York: Harcourt Brace, 1998.

Rubenstein, Saul A., and Thomas A. Kochan. *Learning from Saturn: A Look at the Boldest Experiment in Corporate Governance and Employee Relations.* Ithaca, NY: Cornell University Press, 2001.

Rubin, Jeff. *Why Your World is about to Get a Whole Lot Smaller: Oil and the End of Globalization.* New York: Random House, 2009.

Ryan, William. *Blaming the Victim.* New York: Vintage Press, 1976.

Sachs, Jeffrey. *The Price of Civilization.* New York: Random House, 2011.

Sahlins, Marshall. *Stone Age Economics.* Chicago: Aldine-Atherton, 1972.

Schmitt, Richard. *Introduction to Marx and Engels.* Boulder, CO: Westview Press, 1997.

Schor, Juliet. *The Overworked American: The Unexpected Decline of Leisure.* New York: Basic Books, 1992.

Schweickart, David. *After Capitalism*. Boulder, CO: Westview Press, 1996.

Sennett, Richard. *The Corrosion of Character*. New York: W. W. Norton, 1999.

Service, Elman. *Primitive Social Organization: An Evolutionary Perspective*. New York: Random House, 1968.

Shaxson, Nicholas. *Treasure Islands: Uncovering the Damage of Offshore Banking and Tax Havens*. New York: Macmillan, 2011.

Sherman, Howard. *Reinventing Marxism*. Baltimore: John Hopkins University Press, 1995.

———. *How Society Makes Itself*. Armonk, NY: M. E. Sharpe, 2006.

Sherover-Marcuse, Erica. *Emancipation and Consciousness*. New York: Basil Blackwell, 1986.

Silverstein, Ken. *Washington on $10 Million a Day: How Lobbyists Plunder the Nation*. Monroe, ME: Common Courage Press, 1998.

Smil, Vaclav. *Energy: A Beginner's Guide*. Oxford: Oneworld, 2006.

Stanton, Elizbeth Cady, Susan B. Anthony, and Matilda Joslyn Gage, eds. *The History of Woman Suffrage*. Vol. 1. New York: Fowler and Wells, 1881.

Stone, Douglas, Bruce Patton, and Sheila Heen. *Difficult Conversations*. New York: Penguin Books, 2000.

Stout, Linda. *Bridging the Class Divide*. Boston: Beacon Press, 1996.

Sweezy, Paul, et al. *The Transition from Feudalism to Capitalism.* London: Humanities Press, 1976.

Tainter, Joseph. *The Collapse of Complex Societies.* New York: Cambridge Univ. Press, 1990.

Tawney, R. H. *Religion and the Rise of Capitalism.* London: Hesperides Press, 2006.

Toffler, Alvin. *Future Shock.* New York: Bantam Press, 1970.

Turnbull, Colin. *The Forest People.* New York: Simon & Schuster, 1987.

Van En, Robyn. *Basic Community-Supported Agriculture.* US Department of Agriculture, 1992. http://www.nal.usda.gov/afsic/pubs/csa/csafarmer.shtml

Washburn, Jennifer. *University, Inc: The Corporate Corruption of Higher Education.* New York: Basic Books, 2005.

Wendlinger, Robert. *The Memory Triggering Book.* Oakland, CA: Proust Press, 1995.

Wenke, Robert J. *Patterns in Prehistory.* New York: Oxford University Press, 1990.

Williams, Eric. *Capitalism and Slavery.* Chapel Hill, NC: University of North Carolina Press, 1994.

Wolf, Michael. *Where We Stand. Can America Make it in the Global Race for Wealth and Happiness?* New York: Bantam Books, 1992.

Wolff, Richard. *Capitalism Hits the Fan: The Global Economic Meltdown and What to Do about It.* New York: Olive Branch Press, 2009.

———. *Democracy at Work: A Cure for Capitalism.* Chicago: Haymarket Books, 2012.

Wood, Ellen Meiksins. *Empire of Capital.* New York: Verso Books, 2003.

———. *The Retreat from Class.* London: Verso Books, 1986.

———. *The Origin of Capitalism.* New York: Monthly Review, 1999.

Wright, Ronald. *A Short History of Progress.* New York: Carroll & Graff, 2004.

Yates, Michael D. *Naming the System: Inequality and Work in the Global Economy.* New York: Monthly Review, 2003.

———. *Why Unions Matter.* New York: Monthly Review, 1998.

Zinn, Howard. *A People's History of the United States.* New York: Harper Collins, 1980.

Zweig, Michael. *The Working Class Majority.* Ithaca, NY: Cornell University Press, 2000.

———. *What's Class Got to Do with It?* Ithaca, NY: Cornell University Press, 2004.

INDEX

A

Affluent Society xxii
Afghanistan 110
agriculture 14, 49, 63, 92, 100, 115
Allen, Theodore William 69
Alperovitz, Gar viii
American Federation of Labor 83
American Legislative Exchange Council 53
anthrax 74
Argentina 95, 129, 187, 193
Aristophanes 48

B

Bacon's Rebellion 69
Bardacke, Frank 63
Bari, Judy 114
Barry Commoner 197
Baudrillard, J 108
Blackburn, Robin 70
Blackmon, Douglas A. 70
blue collar 8
Brecht, Bertolt 75
Buckley v. Valeo 56

C

Calvinism 19
capitalism xxii, 8, 16, 37, 58, 74, 87, 109, 138, 195, 197, 198
capitalist class 44, 81, 90, 132, 136
Capitalist Ruling Class 96
Catabolic Capitalism 103
Chin, Vincent 97
Chisholm, Shirley xx
Chomsky, Noam 54
Citizens United 56
civil rights 70, 89
class xv, xxi, 19, 37, 53, 63, 79, 110, 121, 189, 190, 192
class analysis xvi, 4, 35, 61, 79, 125
class struggle xx, 9, 100
class war 86, 87
climate change 108
Cohen, Leonard 50
Collins, Craig vii
Commodity production 19
Commoner, Barry 99, 116, 117
Conner, Clifford D 48

173

consumerism 15, 34, 42
Cooley, Mason 65
coordinators 38
Coordinators 39
core 18, 94
corporate class 93
Corporations 52
Cuba 114

D

Darrow, Clarence 80
Debs, Eugene V xv, 50
deindustrialized xxii
Detroit xxii, 97, 107
Didion, Joan 29
Domhoff, William 51
Du Boff, Richard 76
Du Bois, W.E.B. 68

E

ecological catastrophe 113
Ehrenreich, Barbara 65, 74
Einstein, Albert 31
Ellison, Ralph 67
Energy 102
EROEI 109

F

feminism 130
field slaves 39
Fitzgerald, Francis 6
Fitzgerald, F. Scott 71
fossil fuels 101, 102
Friedman, Milton 94, 123

G

Glass-Steagall Act 134
globalization 91

Goldman, Emma 79
Government 53
green capitalism 117

H

Hamilton, Alexander 18
Harvest of Shame 64
Hawkin, Paul 116
Hayek, Friedrich 94
Heinberg, Richard 106
Hill, Joe 113
Hin, Lee Sui 80
Homer 72
house slaves 39

I

immigrants 63
individualism 7, 11, 44, 62
industrialism 14
industrial revolution 69, 76, 92, 100, 101, 106
International Energy Agency 111
International Labor Organization 32
International monetary fund 94
International Workers of the World 83

J

James, Selma 67
Jay, John 56
Johnson, Daniel 80

K

Kelber, Harry 88
King Jr., Martin Luther 67
Klare, Michael 99, 107
Klein, Naomi 87, 123, 128, 138

L

labor power 5, 9, 17, 21, 83, 127
Leacock, Eleanor 36
legal system 56
LeGrande, Frank 63
Leonard-Wright, Betsy 25
Liebknecht, Karl 126
Lincoln, Abraham 10
Lipsitz, George 77
Loewen, James 6
Luntz, Frank 7

M

Mandela, Nelson 91
Marcuse, Herbert 41
Marmot, Michael 11
Marshall plan 105
Marshall Plan 77, 130
Martin, Judith 11
Marx, Karl 10, 17, 33, 136, 165
McKibben, Bill 118
McLuhan, Marshall 108
means of production 7, 26, 83
media 58, 137
Media 164
Merrill, Michael 5
middle class 38, 41, 125
Modragon 116

N

Nader, Ralph 117
NAFTA 55, 95, 96, 193
neoliberal 94, 95
neoliberalism 93
Neumann, Osha vii

O

Obama administration 125
Occupy Wall Street 40, 137
Onesimus 48
OPEC 105
Orwell, George 38
outsourcing 106
owners xxi

P

Parenti, Michael 75
Patriot Act 57
Peak Oil 105
Pearl Harbor 104
periphery 18, 92, 94
Plato 48, 71, 72, 168
political parties 54
Posse Comitatus act 57
poverty xvi, 31, 32, 95, 116, 197
precariat 8
Primary economy 102, 125, 135
primitive accumulation 17
privatization 17, 31, 59, 87, 93
production process xxi, 15, 24, 35, 72, 73, 94
profit 16, 21, 22, 35, 53, 61, 85, 101, 107, 118, 129, 145, 180
proletarian 8

R

racism 29, 49, 64
rise of slavery 17
Roman Empire 110
Roubini, Nouriel 137
Rubin, Jeff 137
ruling class 50

175

S

Savio, Mario 113
schools 30, 59, 75
Secondary Economy 103
semi-periphery 18, 92
serfs 14, 21, 40, 47, 78, 100
sexism 29, 49, 69
Sherover-Marcuse, Erica vii
Sinclair, Upton xvii, 108
slave trade 70
Smith, Adam 50
social class xix
Socrates xv
Spartacus 78
Stalingrad 104
status 11
Steinbeck, John 43
Stevenson, Walter 34
Stiglitz, Joseph 123
Stone, Oliver 129
Stout, Linda 27
Structural adjustment 95
Structural Adjustment 95
surplus value 16, 39, 143

T

Taft-Hartley act 77
Tainter, Joseph 109
Taylor, Fredrick 72
Tertiary economy 103, 126, 132
Thales 46
The Arab Spring 110
The Iliad 72
Thersites 72
Think tanks 57
TINA 94
Tomlin, Lilly 60
transition town movement 114
tribal society 49, 71

U

Unions xxii, 77, 82, 88, 193
U.S. Labor against the war 97

V

Voltaire 29

W

Wallerstein, Immanuel 25
Warren, Elizabeth 32
Weil, Simone xv
white privilege 68
white race 69
Williams, Eric 69
Wisconsin 86, 88
witches 69
Wolff, Rick 131
Women and children 18
workers xxi
working class 11, 45, 73, 83, 95, 113, 132, 138
World Bank 53, 94
WPA 55

Z

Zapatista 96
Zencey, Eric 138
Zinn, Howard xvii, 76
Zweig, Michael 6

ENDNOTES

Introduction

1. www.tomdispatch.com/post/2003/howard_zinn_the_missing_voices_of_our_world.
2. The following are three excerpted questions from the "social class questionnaire," which is based on a questionnaire used at the Center for Working Life, Oakland, California. The complete version is in appendix 2.
3. Wendlinger, *The Memory Triggering Book*.
4. Few of the images of the workers that I observed contained women or people of color, whereas the beautiful people where composed of both white men and women: men as figures of power and women as decorations.
5. Martin, *Framed!*
6. www.thirdworldtraveler.com/Zinn/CampaignWithoutClass.html.
7. Kawachi, *The Health of Nations*; Milanovic, *Worlds Apart*.
8. McCarthy, *Polarized America*.

Chapter 1

1. Perelman, *The Invention of Capitalism*; Dowd, *Capitalism and Its Economics*.
2. Markets have existed throughout history but only peripherally to the precapitalist systems of production.

3. http://www.truth-out.org/news/item/15655-labor-report-four-major-tv-news-networks-ignore-unions
4. See www.laborheritage.org, www.lib.washington.edu/mcnews/ngl/
5. http://faculty.plattsburgh.edu/richard.robbins/legacy/anth_web_resources.html.
6. www.marxists.org/glossary/frame.htm.
7. Marx and Engels, *The Collected Works of Karl Marx and Frederick Engels*, 6, 476.
8. Michael Merrill, "Putting 'Capitalism' in Its Place: A Review of Recent Literature," *William and Mary Quarterly* 52 (April 1995): 322, 326.
9. "The Wealth Divide: The Growing Gap in the United States Between the Rich and the Rest," *Multinational Monitor*, Vol. 24 No. 5 (May 2003). http://multinationalmonitor.org/mm2003/03may/may03interviewswolff.html.
10. http://www.southmountain.com/.
11. See remarks by anthropologist Eleanor Leacock in Engels, *Dialectics of Nature*.
12. Fitzgerald, *America Revised*; Loewen, *Lies My Teacher Told Me*.
13. Zweig, *The Working Class Majority*.
14. www.mediaed.org/videos/CommercialismPoliticsAndMedia/ClassDismissed/
15. http://www.scpr.org/blogs/economy/2011/12/02/3932/frank-luntz-first-rule-capitalism-you-do-not-talk-/.
16. http://www.truth-out.org/news/item/15680-the-question-of-socialism-and-beyond-is-about-to-open-up-in-these-united-states
17. Ollman, *How to Take an Exam and Remake the World*.

Chapter 2

1. National Opinion Research Center, www.norc.uchicago.edu
2. E. Goode, "For Good Health, It Helps to be Rich and Important," *New York Times*, June 1, 1999: 1.
3. Marmot, *Status Syndrome*.
4. The chapter title, "A Working Definition of Class," refers to the fact that the relation between workers and capitalists changes as society changes.
5. Dalphin, *The Persistence of Social Inequality in America*.
6. David Moberg, "Class Matters," *In These Times*. June 30, 2006.
7. Anthropologist Elman Service proposed a typology of societies composed of bands, tribes, chiefdoms, and states. Service, *Primitive Social Organization*.
8. Marx, *Capital Vol. 1*, chapter 31.
9. Wood, *The Origin of Capitalism*.
10. Mielants, *The Origins of Capitalism and the "Rise of the West."*
11. Blackburn, *The Making of New World Slaver*.
12. http://libcom.org/history/destructive-origins-capitalismrobert-kurz
13. http://www.fordham.edu/halsall/mod/Wallerstein.asp
14. Claudia Goldin and Kenneth Sokoloff, "Women, Children, and Industrialization in the Early Republic: Evidence from the Manufacturing Censuses," *Journal of Economic History* 42 (December 1982): 773.
15. Hamilton, cited in Jones, *American Work*, 161; *Niles' Weekly Register*, June 7, 1817: 227. Also see Thomas Dublin, *Women at Work: The Transformation of Work and Community in Lowell, Massachusetts, 1826–1860*. New York: Columbia University, 1993. http://www.common-place.org/vol-07/no-01/reviews/fichter.shtml.

16. http://pubs.socialistreviewindex.org.uk/isj102/harman.htm#17
17. Tawney, *Religion and the Rise of Capitalism*.
18. Humphries, *Childhood and Child Labour in the British Industrial Revolution*.
19. See Kovel, *The Enemy of Nature*, for a devastating attack on the profit motive, especially chapter 3 about the tragedy at Bhopal, India, killing thousands of people and injuring five hundred thousand; and see also Merchant, *Radical Ecology*.
20. Ibid.
21. Ellison, *Taking the War Out of Our Words*; Edwards, *The Compassionate Revolution*.
22. Leondar-Wright, *Class Matters*.
23. I place quotes around "middle class," because although I disagree with the term, I recognize those who don't hold a class analysis commonly use it.
24. ClassMatters.org
25. Stout, *Bridging the Class Divide*.
26. Wood, *The Retreat from Class*, 68.
27. Sennett, *Corrosion of Character*; Ollman, *Alienation*; Marcuse, *One Dimensional Man*; Parenti, *Democracy for the Few*.

Chapter 3

1. For an extensive bibliography of the relationship between the working class and education, see www.as.ysu.edu/~cwcs/Bibliography.htm and Bowles, *Schooling in Capitalist America*.
2. In *Lies My Teacher Told Me* (202–213), James Loewen describes how ignoring the condition of the working class negatively impacts students.
3. http://cuip.uchicago.edu/~cac/nlu/fnd504/anyon.htm

4. Schor, *The Overworked American*, 29.
5. http://www.swt.org/timeday/degraafnyt0403.htm
6. Before class society, some of the tribal groups worked much less, on average, than we do today and had more leisure time. According to Marshall Sahlins in *Stone Age Economics*, hunter-gatherers consume less energy per capita per year than any other group of human beings. Yet when you come to examine it, the original affluent society was none other than the hunters in which all the people's material wants were easily satisfied. To accept that hunters are affluent is therefore to recognize that the present human condition of people slaving to bridge the gap between unlimited wants and insufficient means is a tragedy of modern times.
7. De Graaf, *Take Back Your Time*.
8. Elizabeth Cady Stanton, Susan Brownell Anthony, Matilda Joslyn Gage, Ida Husted. *History of Woman Suffrage, Volume 1*
9. Bernays, *Propaganda*.
10. Nicholas Wade, "Evolution: Supremacy of a Social Network," *New York Times*, March 14, 2011.
11. Griffin, *Animal Minds*; http://forhumanliberation.blogspot.com/2011/07/456-tool-using-dolphin-finds-fare-on.html
12. Engels, *Dialectics of Nature*, 289.

Chapter 4

1. In some cases, traditional workers (e.g., plumbers) receive higher pay than office workers because their unions fought for them effectively, but in general, pay is higher for the middle class.
2. This term was used by Michael Albert on the Znet website as well as in his book *Parecon*.
3. http://www.truthdig.com/report/print/the_careerists_20120723/
4. http://www.monthlyreview.org/301buhle.htm

5. "Meritocracy in America: Ever higher society, ever harder to ascend" http://www.economist.com/world/na/displayStory.cfm?story_id=3518560 http://www.nytimes.com/2012/01/05/us/harder-for-americans-to-rise-from-lower-rungs.html?_r=1&pagewanted=all
6. Wright, *A Short History of Progress*, 124.
7. See Silverstein, *Washington on $10 Million a Day*. Since 2000, the number of registered lobbyists in Washington DC, has more than doubled to 34,759—Jeffrey H. Birnbaum, "The Road to Riches Is Called K Street," *Washington Post*, June 22, 2005.
8. Consciousness raising must go along with action. See chapter 5.
9. Ehrenreich, *Fear of Falling*.
10. For worldwide differences, see. http://www.worldwatch.org/features/vsow/2003/11/12/. For differences in the United States, see David Wessel, "As Rich-Poor Gap Widens in U.S., Class Mobility Stalls," *Wall Street Journal*, Friday, May 13, 2005. http://www.nytimes.com/2012/01/05/us/harder-for-americans-to-rise-from-lower-rungs.html?pagewanted=all.
11. Bardhan, *Research Report Fisher Center for Real Estate and Urban Economics*. http://64.233.161.104/search?q=cache:y5ibeaDts84J:www.haas.berkeley.edu/news/Research_Report_Fall_2003.pdf+%22new+wave+of+outsourcing%22+haas&hl=en.
12. Ron and Anil Hira, "Outsourcing America," www.washingtontimes.com/commentary/20050423-104818-2947r.htm.
13. http://www.pbs.org/newshour/bb/health/jan-june99/doctors_6-24.html.
14. http://theamericanscholar.org/blue-collar-brilliance/.
15. See "Class Dismissed: How TV Frames the Working Class," a DVD, from the Media Education Foundation, 2006.
16. Readers should not assume that this is an advocacy for a

return to a type of primitive communism. This is merely a recognition that we may learn from an earlier holistic perspective.

Chapter 5

1. Zweig, *The Working Class Majority*, 19.
2. http://sociology.ucsc.edu/whorulesamerica/domhoff_bibliography.html, http://www.globalresearch.ca/index.php?context=viewArticle&code=PET20070323&articleId=5159, http://www.census.gov/hhes/www/income/income.html
3. http://www.thirdworldtraveler.com/Ruling_Elites/WhoRulesAmericaNow.html
4. www.federalreserve.gov/pubs/oss/oss2/method.html, toomuchonline.org, paywatch.com,
5. www.geocities.com/CapitolHill/1931/secD3.html
6. www.freepress.net/ownership/chart/main
7. Chomsky, *Necessary Illusions*; www.mediachannel.org/ownership; www.mediachannel.org/ownership/front.shtml.
8. Edwards, *Burning All Illusions*; Parenti, *Inventing Reality*.
9. For a more extensive discussion of the ruling-class institutions, I suggest to turn to Kivel, *You Call This a Democracy?*; Domhoff, *Who Rules America*; and Parenti, *Democracy for the Few*.
10. David Korten, "When Corporations Rule the World," http://www.uoregon.edu/~vburris/whorules/index.htm.
11. Bakan, *The Corporation*.
12. Perrow, *Organizing America*; http://www.thecorporation.com/index.cfm?page_id=46.
13. Johnston, *The Fine Print: How Big Companies Use Plain English to Rob You Blind*.
14. Clements, *Corporations Are Not People*.

15. www.thirdworldtraveler.com//Controlling_Corporations/Challenge_Corp_Personhood.html
16. In January 2010, the US Supreme Court removed restrictions on some types of corporate spending in support of (or in opposition to) specific candidates. This expanded the free speech rights of corporations.
17. http://reclaimdemocracy.org/personhood/index.html.
18. http://www.globalissues.org/article/59/corporate-power-facts-and-stats.
19. http://siteresources.worldbank.org/INTUWM/Resources/WorldsTop100Economies.pdf.
20. http://www.financialweek.com/apps/pbcs.dll/article?AID=/20081015/REG/8.
21. http://www.aflcio.org/corporatewatch/ns09222004.cfm.
22. Shaxson, *Treasure Islands*.
23. http://www.commondreams.org/archive/2008/04/01/8023.
24. Domhoff, *Who Rules America?*
25. http://alecexposed.org/wiki/What_is_ALEC%3F.
26. Bill Moyer, "The United States of ALEC," http://www.democracynow.org/seo/2012/9/27/the_united_states_of_alec_bill.
27. http://www.truth-out/print/11778.
28. http://www.opensecrets.org/pres08/index.php.
29. Johnson, *Nemesis*, 137.
30. http://www.swans.com/library/art9/melman01.html. Costofwar.org.
31. http://www.washingtonpost.com/world/national-security/petraeus-scandal-puts-four-star-general-lifestyle-under-scrutiny/2012/11/17/33a14f48-3043-11e2-a30e-5ca76eeec857_story.html.
32. http://www.opednews.com/populum/linkframe.php?linkid=155181.

33. http://www.democracynow.org/2004/11/3/nader_blasts_two_party_system.
34. http://topics.nytimes.com/topics/reference/timestopics/organizations/c/commission_on_presidential_debates/index.html.
35. David Cay Johnston, author of *Free Lunch*, mentioned in an interview with Rachel Maddow on December 29, 2008, that our legislators don't get access to working class people. He interviewed all one hundred senators and found only one, Ted Stevens of Alaska, had any access from the working class.
36. Silverstein, *Washington on $10 Million a Day*. Since 2000, the number of registered lobbyists in Washington, DC, has more than doubled to 34,759. Jeffrey H. Birnbaum, "The Road to Riches Is Called K Street," *Washington Post*, June 22, 2005.
37. http://www.opensecrets.org/pfds/index.php.
38. http://www.counterpunch.org/2013/04/19/our-missing-left-opposition/.
39. http://www.nyu.edu/projects/ollman/docs/class.php.
40. Beard, *An Economic Interpretation of the Constitution of the United States*; http://www.thirdworldtraveler.com/America/America's_Blinders.html; Ollman, *Toward a Marxist Interpretation of the Constitution*; http://www.nyu.edu/projects/ollman/docs/us_constitution.php.
41. http://www.campaignfinancesite.org/court/buckley.html.
42. http://yalelawjournal.org/the-yale-law-journal-pocket-part/constitutional-law/citizens-united-and-its-critics/.
43. Reiman, *The Rich Get Richer and the Poor Get Prison*.
44. http://reconstruction.eserver.org/042/swartz.htm.
45. http://www.laborresearch.org/union_busting_watch.php.
46. http://theamericaninjusticesystem.blogspot.com/2008/06/enemy-of-working-class.html.
47. https://www.prisonlegalnews.org/default.aspx.

48. http://www.ojp.usdoj.gov/bjs/prisons.htm, Prison Policy Initiative, PO Box 127, Northampton, MA 01061.
49. http://www.aclu.org/reform-patriot-act.
50. "Whoever, except in cases and under circumstances expressly authorized by the Constitution or Act of Congress, willfully uses any part of the Army or the Air Force as a Posse Comitatus or otherwise to execute the laws shall be fined under this title or imprisoned not more than two years, or both."—Title 18, US Code, Section 1385
51. http://truth-out.org/opinion/item/13546-drone-strikes-are-causing-child-casualties.
52. http://www.nytimes.com/2011/12/04/sunday-review/have-american-police-become-militarized.html?pagewanted=all.
53. Washburn, *University, Inc.*; Aronowitz, *The Knowledge Factory*.
54. Rich, *Think Tanks, Public Policy, and the Politics of Expertise*. In 1970, Supreme Court Justice Powell wrote to the National Chamber of Commerce saying that students are becoming anti-business due to the Vietnam War. He further suggested that rich conservatives to set up professorships and institutes on and off campus where intellectuals would publish conservative books and articles and also set up think tanks.
55. Domhoff, *Who Rules America?*; Dye, *Who's Running America?*
56. http://www.prwatch.org/search/node/%22ruling+class%22, http://www.progressiveliving.org/mass_media_and_politics.htm.
57. http://columbus.indymedia.org/node/13713.
58. Martin, *Framed!*
59. McChesney, *Digital Disconnect*.
60. Bowles, *Schooling in Capitalist America*.
61. Ibid.
62. Cookson, *Preparing for Power*.

63. http://mrzine.monthlyreview.org/wolff170207p.html.
64. Sachs, *The Price of Civilization*.
65. Domhoff, *Bohemian Grove and Other Retreats*; Robbins, *Secrets of the Tomb*.
66. Hayes, *Twilight of the Elites*.
67. http://truth-out.org/video/item/10290-bill-fletcher-jr-and-stephen-lerner-unions-are-in-peril
68. Shaxson, *Treasure Islands*. http://www.truth-out.org/opinion/item/15726-its-time-to-shine-a-light-on-the-poverty-creation-industry
69. Although the most widely used and Small Business Association–endorsed size for small businesses is that the business must have no more than five hundred employees for most manufacturing and mining industries and no more than $7 million in average annual receipts for most nonmanufacturing industries, we will assume that our discussion refers to business of a dozen or so employees.
70. In Argentina, http://americas.irc-online.org/am/3158; in Spain, http://www.iisd.org/50comm/commdb/list/c13.htm, Internationally www.cooponline.coop/about_international.html; in the United States, http://www.coopamerica.org/.
71. "Family Business Shut Their Doors When Wal-Mart Comes to Town," www.aflcio.org/corporatewatch/walmart/walmart_4.cfm.
72. www.kauffman.org/research.cfm?itemID=667.

Chapter 6

1. http://delmarhistory8.wikispaces.com/file/view/Slaves+vs.+Indentured+Servants.pdf.
2. An excluded worker is a worker who is excluded—by either policy or practice—from the right to organize and other crucial labor rights and protections. http://excludedworkers.org/what.

3. http://en.wikipedia.org/wiki/National_Labor_Relations_Act.
4. Under Cesar Chavez, some farm workers were organized but since his death have become a less powerful force; see Bardacke, *Trampling Out the Vintage*.
5. http://motherjones.com/politics/2008/07/what-do-prisoners-make-victorias-secret.
6. http://cheapmotelsandahotplate.org/2012/02/23/slavery-by-another-name/.
7. http://www.un.org/apps/news/story.asp?NewsID=43892&Cr=labour&Cr1=#.UO5Zx0Z4SXA.
8. Hochschild, *Global Woman*.
9. Rothernberg, *With These Hands*, 117.
10. Ehrenreich, *Nickel and Dimed*.
11. http://online.wsj.com/article/SB10001424052702303879604577407864232528118.html.
12. "Jobless Recovery Leaves Middle Class Behind," http://www.nytimes.com/2012/04/13/us/13iht-letter13.html?_r=0.
13. http://www.alternet.org/activism/7-amazing-fights-rights-workers.
14. http://topics.nytimes.com/top/reference/timestopics/subjects/t/tea_party_movement/index.html?8qa.
15. http://interoccupy.net/newswire/.
16. Also see definitions in the glossary.
17. Sherover-Marcuse, *Emancipation and Consciousness*, 5, 145.
18. Roediger, *The Wages of Whiteness*.
19. http://www.amptoons.com/blog/files/mcintosh.html.
20. http://www.freireproject.org/content/web-du-bois-1868-1963-0.
21. Federici, *Caliban and the Witch*.
22. http://en.wikipedia.org/wiki/Bacon's_Rebellion.
23. Williams, *Capitalism and Slavery*.
24. Blackburn, *The Making of New World Slavery*.
25. Blackmon, *Slavery by Another Name*.

26. See the PBS documentary "Slavery by Another Name," http://video.pbs.org/program/slavery-another-name/,
27. Homer, *Iliad*, book ii, 211–78.
28. In the 1920s, Taylorism was supplemented by Fordism, the introduction of a moving assembly line into the auto plants, where workers further lost control of their work pace and had to adjust to the speed of the assembly line. This process was carried on to industries in other sectors of American industry. Further advancements in management science where introduced by Frank and Lillian Gilbreth, and later by W. Edwards Deming's total quality management (TQM) that was instrumental in the development of Japan's automobile industry..
29. For an update on this subject, see "Class Dismissed: How TV Frames the Working Class," a DVD from the Media Education Foundation.
30. Noam Chomsky interviewed by Mathew Tempest, *The Guardian*, February 4, 2003.
31. http://truth-out.org/news/item/13990-how-did-the-gates-of-hell-open-in-vietnam.
32. Rose, *The Mind at Work*.
33. Ehrenreich, *Nickel and Dimed*.
34. http://womenborntranssexual.com/2012/07/06/nickel-and-dimed-from-the-american-ruling-class/.
35. Three days after anthrax was discovered in a letter to Senate Majority Leader Tom Daschle, the postmaster general held a news conference to declare that the letter had been well sealed and posed little risk to workers. But by the following Monday, two postal workers were dead, and two others were infected with anthrax.
36. The postal workers' union complained about the slow, sloppy response of authorities to the threat anthrax posed to mail handlers, well after the authorities took stringent measures to protect US senators' offices. Fortunately, the

union's complaint received enough publicity in the mass media and embarrassed the authorities to backtrack and take care of the workers' needs.
37. Gonzalez, *Fallout*.
38. http://www.thenation.com/blog/toxic-air, http://www.globalpost.com/dispatch/news/regions/americas/united-states/110727/911-health-cancer-ground-zero.
39. Countryman, *Americans*.
40. Parenti, *History as Mystery*.
41. Ibid., xi.
42. Ibid., xvi–xvii.
43. Du Boff, *Accumulation and Power*.
44. Lipsitz, *Class and Culture in Cold War America*.
45. Fitzgerald, *America Revised*.
46. In the documentary film *Why We Fight*, Eisenhower's original farewell speech said military-industrial-congressional complex, but some of his staff wanted it removed so as to not offend congress.
47. The Russian Revolution was the most important event of the twentieth century where the working class took power. This revolution was overthrown in the early to mid-1920s by the counterrevolution led by Stalin. But it retained the word "communist" and "working class," thus discrediting the terms in the United States, which was especially focused on the USSR after World War II.
48. Aronowitz, *How Class Works*, 200.

Chapter 7

1. Perelman, *The Invisible Handcuffs of Capitalism*.
2. Jeffrey Pfeffer, "In Praise of Organized Labor," *Business 2.0*, June 2005. http://money.cnn.com/magazines/business2/business2_archive/2005/06/01/8263459/index.htm. An excellent historical view of the transition of the labor

movement is *Stayin' Alive: The 1970s and the Last Days of the Working Class* by Jefferson Cowie (New York: New Press 2010).
3. http://www.epi.org/publications/entry/briefingpapers_bp143/.
4. AFL-CIO Web site http://www.aflcio.org/aboutunions/joinunions/union101.cfm.
5. Moody, *Injury to All*.
6. www.iww.org/stand.shtml.
7. http://www.starbucksunion.org/.
8. http://www.newswise.com/articles/study-union-decline-accounts-for-much-of-the-rise-in-wage-inequality.
9. http://en.wikipedia.org/wiki/Income_inequality_in_the_United_States.
10. http://www.ips-dc.org/articles/tax_day_talking_points.
11. http://blog.buzzflash.com/node/12533.
12. Burns, *Reviving the Strike*.
13. http://www.bls.gov/ces/cesstrk.htm.
14. http://www.alternet.org/activism/7-amazing-fights-rights-workers.
15. http://blog.aflcio.org/2010/10/29/ny-times-nations-labor-laws-weak-and-irrelevant/.
16. Greer, *The Long Descent*, 196.
17. Based in part on his experiences as a corporate lawyer and as a representative for the tobacco industry with the Virginia legislature, Louis Powell wrote a memo to a friend at the US Chamber of Commerce. The memo called for corporate America to become more aggressive in molding politics and law in the United States and may have sparked the formation of one or more influential right-wing think tanks. http://old.mediatransparency.org/story.php?storyID=21.
18. Klein, *The Shock Doctrine*.
19. http://www.truthout.org/international-assault-labor/1304431702.

20. http://www.adbusters.org/blogs/adbusters_blog/citizen_or_consumer.html.
21. Michael Sandel, "What Money Can't Buy: The Moral Limits of Markets." http://bp.baihua.org/user_image2/2011/11/1320205825_1.pdf.
22. Fitch, *Solidarity for Sale.*
23. See www.alec.org, http://www.talk2action.org/story/2011/4/4/142733/1743.
24. http://truth-out.org/opinion/item/13544-the-folly-of-right-to-work.
25. http://www.thenation.com/blogs/lee-fang. For a history of this attack on labor, see "The Racist Roots of 'Right To Work' Laws," by Chris Kromm. http://www.southernstudies.org/2012/12/the-racist-roots-of-right-to-work-laws.html; http://truth-out.org/opinion/item/13391-the-conservative-agenda-behind-right-to-work-in-michigan
26. http://www.laboreducator.org/.
27. McAlevey, *Raising Expectations (and Raising Hell).*
28. http://www.thenation.com/article/161978/alec-exposed; http://www.alternet.org/economy/149531/the_class_war_launched_by_america%27s_wealthiest_is_getting_more_savage/.
29. http://www.ilo.org/wcmsp5/groups/public/---dgreports/---dcomm/---publ/documents/publication/wcms_163855.pdf.

Chapter 8

1. http://www.sociology.emory.edu/globalization/theories01.html.
2. Hansen, *The Silk Road.*
3. http://www.fordham.edu/halsall/mod/Wallerstein.asp.
4. Diamond, *Guns, Germs, and Steel.*
5. http://www.colorado.edu/AmStudies/lewis/2010/decline.htm#President.

6. http://www.frontlineonnet.com/fl2105/stories/20040312006011700.htm.
7. http://www.zcommunications.org/problems-of-neoliberalism-by-edward-said.
8. McMurtry, *The Cancer Stage of Capitalism*.
9. http://www.imf.org/external/index.htm.
10. http://www.whirledbank.org/development/sap.html.
11. See *Confessions of an Economic Hit Man* by John Perkins for a readable description of the structural adjustment process. http://www.economichitman.com/.
12. See Joseph Stiglitz, "Argentina, Shortchanged." http://www.argentina-info.net/argentina-_shortchanged.html.
13. http://useconomy.about.com/od/tradepolicy/p/NAFTA_History.htm.
14. William Tabb, "Getting Serious About Class Dynamics: Culture, Politics and Class," New Politics. http://new pol.org.
15. http://www.wto.org/.
16. http://uslaboragainstwar.org/; http://www.iww.org/.
17. Alan Howard, "The Future of Global Unions: Is Solidarity Still Forever?" *Dissent* vol. 54 no. 4 (Fall 2007): 62–70.
18. http://www.opednews.com/articles/US-as-World-Class-Bully-by-Mary-Wentworth-121116-949.html.
19. David Murphy and Charles Hall, *EROI, Insidious Feedbacks, and the End of Economic Growth*. Prepublication, 2010
20. Heinberg, *The End of Growth*, 284–5. Rubin, *Why Your World is about to Get a Whole Lot Smaller*.

Chapter 9

1. Smil, *Energy*; Holmgren, *Future Scenarios*; Kunstler, *The Long Emergency*; Heinberg, *The Party's Over*; Rifkin, *Entropy*; Greer, *The Long Descent*.
2. Barbour, *Energy and American Values*.

3. As early as the late nineteenth century, scientists began the climate disruption debate by pointing out that human caused emissions of greenhouse gases could change the climate.
4. Heinberg, *The Party's Over*.
5. http://www.energybulletin.net/stories/2011-08-01/when-oil-and-gas-are-depleted.
6. http://www.google.com/url?sa=t&rct=j&q=&esrc=s&source=web&cd=3&ved=0CDYQFjAC&url=http%3A%2F%2Ffaculty.washington.edu%2Fgmobus%2FBiophysicalEconomics%2FburkhartReview.pdf&ei=MdtPUIyJDYfgiAKPqYCADg&usg=AFQjCNHB8VCYzh0ZGGHllV0LXKQF4HzmA&sig2=I9_GtyK9TRkzf9IM0N3Nxg.
7. Heinberg, *The Party's Over*.
8. Greer, *The Wealth of Nature*, chapter 2.
9. Biology: a destructive metabolism; the breaking down in living organisms of more complex substances into simpler ones, with the release of energy
10. McNally, *Global Slump*.
11. http://truth-out.org/news/item/10572-meet-catabolic-capitalism globalizations-evil-twin.
12. http://truth-out.org/news/item/11173-cannibalistic-capitalism-and-green-resistance.
13. Greer, *The Long Descent*, 105.
14. http://energybulletin.net/primer.php.
15. http://dissidentvoice.org/2012/09/capitalisms-quagmire/.
16. Barlett, *The Betrayal of the American Dream*.
17. http://thinkprogress.org/economy/2011/04/19/159555/us-corporations-outsourced-americans/.
18. http://reclaimdemocracy.org/corporate_accountability/powell_memo_lewis.html.
19. http://www.guardian.co.uk/business/2010/apr/11/peak-oil-production-supply.
20. http://www.Detropiathefilm.com.

21. http://www.huffingtonpost.com/2012/07/23/austerity-wall-street_n_1690838.html.
22. http://www.truth-out.org/petroleum-junkies-world-unite/1320430060.
23. http://w.w.w.truth-out.org, The Collapse of the Old Oil Order: How the Petroleum Age Will End.
24. Heinberg, *Peak Everything*; Kunstler, *The Long Emergency*.
25. Daly, *Ecological Economics, Second Edition*; Meadows, *Limits to Growth*; Greer, *The Wealth of Nature*, Heinberg, *The End of Growth*.
26. A study commissioned by twenty developing countries is warning more than one hundred million people will die by 2030 if the world fails to take on global warming. The report also warns global warming threatens to seriously contract the global economy over the next decade. http://www.democracynow.org/2012/9/27/headlines/study_global_warming_could_claim_100m_lives_by_2030.
27. Baudrillard, *America*, 51.
28. Mander, *The Capitalism Papers*.
29. Tainter, *The Collapse of Complex Societies*.
30. http://en.wikipedia.org/wiki/Lists_of_disasters.
31. https://mail.google.com/mail/?shva=1#inbox/1395d671227e5829.
32. http://billmoyers.com/segment/chris-hedges-on-capitalism's-'sacrifice-zones'/.
33. Ostrom, *Governing the Commons*; Janssen, *Working Together*.
34. Bakerinstitute.org; The Status of World Oil Reserves: Conventional and Unconventional
35. http://www.sciencedaily.com/releases/2012/02/120222154641.htm.
36. http://www.springer.com/engineering/energy+technology/book/978-1-4419-9397-7.

37. http://independentreport.blogspot.com/2012/03/tar-sands-too-inefficient-energy.html.
38. Charles Hall Provisional Results from EROI Assessments. Theoildrum.com/node/3810.
39. http://www.treehugger.com/natural-sciences/tar-sands-projects-responsible-for-water-pollution-in-albertas-rivers-despite-industry-claims-to-contrary.html.
40. http://online.wsj.com/article/SB10001424127887323894704578114492856065064.html.
41. http://www.ipsnews.net/2011/12/fracking-for-shale-gas-neither-clean-nor-green/.
42. http://www.foodandwaterwatch.org/tools-and-resources/us-energy-insecurity-why-fracking-for-oil-and-natural-gas-is-a-false-solutioneu/.
43. http//www/oildecline.com/.
44. Brenner, *Rebel Rank and File*.
45. See "The Power of Community: How Cuba Survived Peak Oil," A DVD documentary, Community Solution, 2006. http://communitysolution.org/cuba.html. Also, Richard Levins, "How Cuba is Going Ecological," *Capitalism, Nature, Socialism* vol. 16 no. 3 (2005): 7–25.
46. Bari, *Timber Wars*.
47. http://www.umassvegetable.org/food_farming_systems/csa/.
48. http://www.transitionus.org.
49. http://rebuildthedream.com/.
50. http://www.thenation.com/article/160949/new-economy-movement. http://www.community-wealth.org/.
51. http://www.salon.com/2012/05/22/rise_of_the_new_economy_movement/.
52. http://www.peri.umass.edu/; Pollin, *Back to Full Employment*.
53. http://www.nelp.org/
54. http://www.californiagrange.org/.

55. http://www.citizen.org/Page.aspx?pid=2306.
56. http://usworker.coop/front.
57. http://www.youtube.com/watch?v=N1fiubmOqH4; Hawken, *Blessed Unrest*.
58. MacLeod, *From Mondragon to America*.
59. http://www.greenworker.coop/website_j/.
60. Books by Barry Commoner: *The Closing Circle* (1971), *The Poverty of Power*, (1979), *The Politics of Energy* (1979), *Making Peace with the Planet* (1992).
61. Lilley, *Catastrophism*, 58.
62. Bill McKibben, "Global Warming's Terrifying New Math," *Rolling Stone*, July 19, 2012. http://www.rollingstone.com/politics/news/global-warmings-tcrigying-newmathe-20120719.

Appendix 1

1. See Wendlinger, *Triggers*, for excellent techniques to recover lost memories.

Appendix 2

1. Traditionally, capitalists are the owners of the means of production. I will extend that meaning to the bureaucrats who represent the capitalists and conduct the planning and operation of the companies that the capitalists own.
2. http://www.youtube.com/watch?v=N2KLyYKJGk0
3. Feinstein, *The Shadow World*.
4. http://thinkprogress.org/politics/2010/05/28/99838/argentine-prime-bush-war/.
5. http://www.alternet.org/world/41083/?page=1.
6. http://endofcapitalism.com/2009/10/21/peak-oil-and-peak-capitalism-professor-richard-wolff/.
7. Robert E. Yuskavage and Mahnaz Fahim-Nader, "Gross Domestic Product by Industry for 1947–86," *Bureau of*

Economic Analysis, Survey of Current Business (December 2005): 71; US Census Bureau, The 2010 Statistical Abstract, Table 656, "Gross Domestic Product by Industry and State: 2008"; Phillips, *Bad Money*, 31.
8. http://www.chinausatraders.com/blog/wp-content/uploads/2010/12/Share-of-Global-Manufacturing-Output1.jpg, http://midwest.chicagofedblogs.org/archives/2010/08/bill_strauss_mf.html.
9. http://2010.newsweek.com/top-10/history-altering-decisions/clinton-signs-securities-legislation.html.
10. See films like *Inside Job*, *Heist*, and *Capitalism Hits the Fan*.
11. http://monthlyreview.org/2009/11/01/the-paradox-of-wealth-capitalism-and-ecological-destruction.
12. Clive Thomson, "Nothing Grows Forever," *Mother Jones*, http://www.motherjones.com/print/53226.
13. http://www.opednews.com/articles/Michael-Klare-Oil-Wars-on-by-Tom-Engelhardt-120510-971.html.
14. Greer, *The Wealth of Nature*; Heinberg, *The End of Growth*; Meadows, *Limits to Growth*; http://endofcapitalism.com/2009/02/20/peak-oil-root-of-the-economic-crisis/.
15. http://endofcapitalism.com/2010/04/07/the-end-of-growth.
16. http://www.theoildrum.com/node/4727.
17. http://www.economonitor.com/nouriel/2012/03/15/scary-oil/.
18. http://dss.ucsd.edu/~jhamilto/oil_history.pdf.
19. Mander, *The Capitalist Papers*, 7.

CPSIA information can be obtained at www.ICGtesting.com
Printed in the USA
LVOW13s2359190713

343585LV00001B/71/P